NEGOTIATING WITH A BULLY

NEGOTIATING WITH A BULLY

TAKE CHARGE AND TURN THE TABLES ON
PEOPLE TRYING TO PUSH YOU AROUND

GREG WILLIAMS WITH PAT IYER

Foreword by Harvey Mackay, #1 New York Times bestselling author

CAREER
PRESS

This edition first published in 2018 by Career Press, an imprint of
Red Wheel/Weiser, LLC
With offices at:
65 Parker Street, Suite 7
Newburyport, MA 01950
www.redwheelweiser.com
www.careerpress.com

ISBN: 978-1-63265-135-8
Library of Congress Cataloging-in-Publication Data
available upon request.

Cover design by Jeff Piasky
Typeset in Minion Pro and Baskerville

Printed in Canada
MAR
10 9 8 7 6 5 4 3 2 1

Dedication

This book is dedicated to my family, who has provided years of support, understanding, and real-life examples of how someone like me can always bounce back from adversity when surrounded by the insulation from harm that one receives from the love of one's family.

Marie L. Preston—Mother Preston—is a woman who accepted me into her life when I was a teenager and she's been like a mother to me since then. Throughout the years, she helped to shape my life as she guided me along the path of righteousness and insights. I've always felt grateful that God graced me with such a gift. Thus, I wanted to acknowledge God's gift of Mother Preston and say thank you for giving me a gift that has been given to me for so many years.

This book is also dedicated to David and Dina Dadian. David and Dina have been friends in the worst of times and the best of times; David has been and continues to be my brother. When it comes to friendship, David and Dina are two people who I know without a doubt I can call on, no matter the need! I know because it's been tested!

Acknowledgments

I received insights, assistance, and support to write this book from the following people. To each of you, I truly appreciate the value you added to this project.

In addition, I hope those individuals who read this book will be able to use and derive benefits from its content to deal more effectively with bullies. To the readers I'd like to say, "Remember, you're always negotiating."

Pat Iyer (my developmental editor): Pat is a very gifted author in her own right. As a developmental editor she helped make my words and negotiation expertise capture more of the essence that occurs when negotiating with a bully. Thus, without Pat on this project the reader would have ended up with a lot of "how-to's" about negotiation strategies and techniques without the stories and examples to drive the content deeper into the reader's mind.

Michael Snell (my literary agent): If ever you want someone on your team who will fight for you, it's Michael Snell; he's smart and tactical about when to go to battle. Michael is the kind of person you want on your side when it comes to negotiating with others to make sure you see and consider broader perspectives. He's also the person who looks at the picture when you are in the frame and cannot see the whole picture yourself.

Damon Willis (a friend with extraordinary sales training abilities): I had the good fortune of working with Damon when I was associated with the Brendon Burchard organization. I believe God creates environments from which we can be enhanced. Being in that environment allowed me to meet Damon and partake of his extremely knowledgeable insights when it comes to teaching others how to sell better. The one thing that makes his insights about sales even more captivating is that he is someone who genuinely believes in helping others. He's not someone who seeks to manipulate others, rather he seeks to embolden others with the knowledge he imparts.

Yolanda Royster (businesswoman and thought stimulator): I had numerous conversations with Yolanda about the content of this book. At times, she challenged my assertions, which led me to consider new thoughts and ideas. Her perspectives about people in general, and women in particular, allowed me to shift my paradigm at times. Every time I did so, this book became a little better.

Kristin Williams-Washington, PsyD (contributing psychologist): I turned to Dr. Washington to gain more insight into the mental aspects from which bullies engage with others. Throughout our interactions, I found her comprehension on this subject matter to be well thought out, well presented, and of great value. In seeking her professional perspective, she allowed me to better understand a bully's behavior as to what motivates him to take the actions he engages in.

Career Press and Red Wheel/Weiser (my publisher): It is always nice to work with smart people who you can count on to present your work in the best light. Such are the people at Red Wheel/Weiser (formerly Career Press). In working with the people at Career Press on my last book *Body Language Secrets to Win More Negotiations* I discovered the value of working with extremely knowledgeable people in the book publishing industry. For all that you have done and will continue to do to get my work out to a worldwide audience, I very humbly thank you.

Contents

Foreword

Success in life and business dealings is not an accident. It is achieved through planning, execution, and evaluation. Effective communication requires an appropriate amount of skills, sensitivity, and understanding of the needs of others.

Bullies show up in our lives in the form of clients, colleagues, and co-workers. As a culture, we are increasingly aware of the impact of bullies. Bullying behavior complicates effective communication.

Everyone has felt bullied at some point in their lives. The bully could be a family member, childhood acquaintance, colleague, employer, or client. You know you have been bullied when you felt pressured, demeaned, and angered by the bully's behavior. You walked away from a negotiation feeling like you lost ground. You gave into demands and agreed to something that was not in your best interests. And you resented the way you felt.

Negotiating With a Bully will teach you how to skillfully deal with bullies in different forms and environments. You'll explore the mindset of a bully and understand the motivations and behaviors so that you can gain an advantage over the bully.

The destructive effects of bullies complicate communication and damage self-esteem, advancement potential, and peace of mind. The people who can spot a bully and create a dialogue that achieves objectives are going to be the most successful.

Negotiating With a Bully addresses a pervasive behavior in our homes, schools, and workplaces. This book discusses the causes, manifestations, and consequences of bullying behavior. It reveals the ways bullies position themselves in negotiations and arms the reader with the insights needed to combat bullying. In these pages, you will discover how to recognize a bully and respond from a position of power.

What can you expect to gain from this book? *Negotiating With a Bully* will help you prepare to confront and thwart a bully. It will teach you how to gain insight into the thought process of the bully as well as use negotiation strategies to address the bully's behavior. The way you recognize the body language used by bullies allows you to gain control of a situation, so you don't walk away with that sick feeling that you've been railroaded.

Think of this book as a source you can turn to for better results in any negotiation with a bully. Through absorbing the stories and tips, you will gain greater confidence when interacting with a bully. This book will be your silent shield so you can disarm a bully's tactics and threats.

I applaud Greg Williams for tackling a difficult subject and giving practical guidance on how to negotiate with a bully.

—Harvey Mackay, *New York Times* #1 bestselling author of *Swim With the Sharks Without Being Eaten Alive*

1

Recognizing Bullies

Bullying behavior is on the rise. It has invaded schools, homes, work settings. and politics. After the 2016 U.S. presidential election, we've seen normalizing of bullying behavior, particularly directed at women and minorities. During that election the slogan "Make America Great Again" was an ambiguous message that some have interpreted as a call to return to a time when wages were higher and jobs were more secure. Others interpret the slogan as coded racial language designed to signal a rollback to a time when people of color (and women) knew their place.[1] When Bill Clinton was campaigning for his wife in 2016, he commented about the slogan: "If you're a white Southerner, you know exactly what it means, don't you?"[2]

Now we see the results of a message some interpret as having racial overtones. The 2017 Charlottesville, Virginia, incident originated from a person identified as a white supremacist. He started a chain collision that resulted in a person being killed by a car at a protest.[3] We have seen white police officers caught on camera saying, "We only shoot black folks. Don't worry about it. You're white. You're okay."[4]

There is an increase in incidents of race-related bullying. Some people have been emboldened to unleash their prejudices. One of my colleagues knows a woman who is a peace center coordinator. She reports a tremendous increase in the number of requests for assistance for supporting churches, schools, individuals, or community groups because of the rise in anti-Semitism and racism.

The peace center coordinator shared a story of arranging a candlelight vigil to take place outside a senator's office. Before the event, the senator called the peace center coordinator to say he felt bullied because there would be people outside of his office. She explained that people participating in a candlelight vigil was well within their rights and that it wasn't bullying. He said, "If you don't stop this, I can shut you down." She said, "Now that is bullying. Do you understand the difference between a candlelight vigil and threatening to shut us down?" Contrast that with the white supremist candlelight vigil march that occurred the night before the horrific car incident and you get a sense of why bullying is open to interpretation.

This story highlights the need to clarify the difference between a bullying incident and a non-bullying incident. The difference between bullying and negotiation is perception—the perspective someone has about bullying. In the example of the peace center coordinator, the senator wanted to position a peaceful demonstration as bullying to intimidate the coordinator. In the case of the white supremist march on the college campus, there was a harkening back to the days when the Ku Klux Klan marched with its torches and white crosses burning. Those actions were intended to be intimidating. The same signal intent was meant to be conveyed at the Charlottesville march. The actions you perceive as bullying are open to interpretation and your perception.

BULLY TYPES

A bully is "a blustering, browbeating person; *especially*: one who is habitually cruel, insulting, or threatening to others who are weaker, smaller, or in some way vulnerable."[5]

A bully acts in a physically or verbally aggressive manner and can be overly aggressive by standing too close to someone; the tone of their conversation and the words they use convey their sentiments. "I will kill you" as opposed to "I'm going to kick your butt" could be one form of bullying that's displayed in the word choice. The former choice is aggressive, whereas the latter is a softer choice.

Bullies can be categorized into three distinct types based on their behavior:

The *hardcore* bully is someone who likely had psychological challenges as a child. This bully wants the respect and acknowledgement that he is someone to reckon with. The hardcore bully takes the attitude that "If you don't give me what I want I may beat your brains in." These are dangerous individuals who may end up in correctional facilities for assault or murder. The hardcore bully stands out because the bullying behavior is so flagrant and easily identifiable.

The *middlecore* bully is someone who might be a bully based on a set of circumstances. Although all bullies seek to maximize their bullying efforts based on situational opportunities, the middlecore bully is someone who has graduated from being a softcore bully and, if allowed, will seek to escalate his efforts to become a hardcore bully.

The *softcore* bully is a bully in training. In some cases, the person will attempt to bully others based on the environment: who is with him and what is occurring. Bullying behavior may be triggered by the dynamics of a situation in which a person who is not ordinarily a bully will take a bully position. Bullying behavior typically occurs out of feelings of helplessness or the need for attention. When individuals are placed in a situation where they feel helpless, they may lash out at those around them in an attempt to assert some semblance of power or control. Additionally, individuals may simply want to feel or present themselves as more powerful, lofty, or deserving than others and may assert these presumed attributes by belittling those around them.[6]

Knowledge of the bully's type helps you understand how to use brain games (negotiation strategies). If you're negotiating with any one of those three types, you would use different negotiation tactics and strategies for each.

SOCIOPATHS

A sociopath is an individual with a diagnosable personality disorder (antisocial personality disorder) who displays antisocial behaviors and has a lack of or highly questionable moral compass. This individual is superficial and incapable of establishing meaningful relationships and connections with others, lacks empathy, displays impulsivity and unreliability, is incapable of accepting responsibility for his or her actions, and displays a complete disregard for rules. This person cares only for him- or herself. Sociopaths cannot be diagnosed as such until they are at least 18 years old, but personality traits must have persisted since age 15. There are a host of reasons that an individual can become a sociopath. There are both biological (nature) and environmental (nurture) theories that can attribute to the progression of the personality disorder. Biologically, there are theories that postulate that the brains of sociopaths develop at a slower rate and that early brain damage can be a factor. Environmentally, early experiences of trauma, rejection, abuse, and extreme poverty can all be causes, as can other adverse early childhood experiences.[5]

A sociopath displays bullying behavior such as physical abuse, publicly humiliating the target, deliberately hurting others to achieve goals, and overreacting to minor offenses. If they are challenged or confronted about it, they will blame others.[7]

THE SHIFT OF POWER

Bullying takes place within the context of who is in power. For example, in the United States there are a lot of older white males in political power, but the demographics are also shifting away from the dominance of white males. There are more minorities, people from other countries, and those who have English as a second language. More women are going into higher education and coming out with advanced degrees, and more women are going into medical school and law school than men. Increasing numbers of women are running for political offices as well. This shift of power affects a negotiation and will increasingly do so as the demographics continue to erode the white male's power base from both a control perspective (that is, the bully determines when and how things are done) and a financial perspective. The awareness of the loss of power is a trigger for bullying.

Let me be clear: I am not implying that most white males are bullies. Only a few are. Of those who are, you need to know which classification you are dealing with (hardcore, middlecore, or softcore). Be mindful to not offer opportunities for a less consistent bully to escalate in behavior. When people feel threatened they will do something to protect their position no matter what their ethnicity is. Feeling threatened in a negotiation may lead to aggressive behavior.

Suppose the other negotiator has had power throughout his life to do whatever he wanted. Is that bullying if he uses the same power today that he used 20 years ago? It might be, given societal changes. In a negotiation, you should also consider how your actions in dealing with a bully today will be viewed in the future. Your actions today may brand you as tomorrow's bully. If the other negotiators feel threatened, and a lot of those in that demographic feel as though their power base or source is being threatened, they're going to respond. Powerful people:

1. Try to maintain that power.
2. Attempt to enhance it to the degree that they can.
3. Do whatever is required, including cheating and stealing, to maintain their power base.

A powerful person who does not feel threatened is likely to be a reasonable negotiator. When he does feel threatened, it behooves you to allay his fears about you and the threat you may present when you're in a negotiation. Understand his mindset: "I've always had power. I'm not going to give it up easily." (That's how revolutions come about.) This attitude may result in you having to revolt to disrupt the negotiation and take the power away from the other negotiator.

Power is the assumption of what one can do in a situation based on the degree of power that someone else allows a person to possess. Anyone, especially in a negotiation, is only as powerful as the opposing negotiator allows that person to be.

I had a situation like that once with an automobile dealer. He felt as though he could force me into agreeing to a sale. He said, "Here's the pen, sign on the dotted line. I know you don't have any questions. It is time to sign." He thought he was in a power position. Instead of signing on the dotted line, I got up and walked out. I refused to allow him to have that power over me.

SEXUAL PREDATORS

Sexual predators are found in settings in which the bully has power over others: in religion, politics, prisons, the entertainment industry, news stations, health care, and so on. A sexual predator is a person seen as obtaining or trying to obtain sexual contact with another person in a metaphorically "predatory" or abusive manner. They act in a way that is analogous to how a predator hunts down its prey, so the sexual predator is thought to "hunt" for his or her sex partners.[8]

A sexual predator may act as a bully in the pursuit of the prey. One type of sexual predator seeks women. Depending on the culture women are supposed to be more docile than their male counterparts. That culture can set the standards whereby a bully could become a sexual predator because the woman is supposed to be submissive. In some situations, the woman is expected to be subservient to the demands of the man, even if the attention is unwanted. When a woman needs what a man is offering, that's when she places herself into an even weaker position. You can keep this scenario in mind as an example when negotiating; when you think about wanting the outcome of a negotiation too much and if you desperately need what the other negotiator has you can potentially place yourself in a weakened position.

A sense of shame plays a crucial role in the way the prey will choose to act. Typically, the woman feels isolated when a man is using sexual attention or makes demands that she does not want. She feels that if she stands up against this man she stands alone, and thus she has no leverage. It's not until leverage is used in the form of multiple women coming out against the situation that we see change.

Prior to the 2016 election, the future president of the United States, Donald Trump, was caught making statements about being able to grab a woman's genitalia. Several women related incidents that confirmed his boasts. But the backlash went against those women because of the support that the candidate had. He demeaned women with statements such as, "Look at her. Do you think I would want to do something with her?"

Making such accusations about a woman's appearance demeans her further. It raises questions about her truthfulness and willingness to speak out. What could she possibly gain by making false accusations? Is she really that unattractive? How does that affect her self-esteem? In a negotiation you should be mindful of your words and the effect they may have on the negotiation.

In some cases, men who are in power have a way of getting back at the women not in power or who they abuse sexually in the form of being able to either give them promotions or have them fired.

For example, the concept of the "casting couch" in the movie industry is based on the dynamic of powerful men demanding sexual favors in exchange for acting parts for women. In 2017, the Hollywood code of silence was broken by women who came forward with their stories about studio executive Harvey Weinstein. He was accused of being a bully and sexual predator. He has been accused of groping and raping women, forcing a woman to perform oral sex, masturbating in front of a woman, asking women for massages when he was nude, for women to take a bath with him, take off their clothes for him, and more. His behavior dates back decades.[9]

Harvey Weinstein used his power to help actresses become stars in their industry or at the very least get roles in certain movies. Those who risked saying no to his advances had to think of the repercussions on their career. Kate Beckinsale was one who said no. She "continued to turn the producer down professionally for years" and said her career was "undoubtedly harmed."[10] Rosanna Arquette refused to give him a massage or touch his penis, telling him she would "never do that." She feels her career was damaged because of it. "He made things very difficult for me for years."[11]

Women in the entertainment industry were aware of his power but some were unprepared for what they encountered when they met with Mr. Weinstein; they thought they were there to talk about a part rather than be treated as prey. They did not have an opportunity to consider, "If I go into this environment what body language signals should I convey to show I will not submit to his demands? What should I be watching for as a signal to tell me it's time to get out? Who else should I take into the environment with me so that the man will not put himself into a position of bullying me?"

Women are sometimes blamed for whatever has happened to them. ("She was 'asking for it' before she was raped.") This accusation sends a signal to other women who might come forward that this is going to happen to them. Women must be mindful of the position they place themselves in and then keep themselves in when it comes to sexual harassment and bullying. Staying in the situation as opposed to leaving it whenever possible, and keeping quiet about what has occurred allows the sexual predator to continue.

Women who set off an alarm about the predator's actions must be willing to pay a price to do so. The price can be extremely high depending on the environment and the situation. It can be a loss of employment, respect, or reputation. It affects women in a vast variety of industries. It is not limited to show business, politics, or anywhere else. It is a difficult problem to tackle because it is pervasive and requires women to speak up to challenge the power structure of the male environment—an environment that allows and endorses this kind of behavior.

The power to confront a bully or sexual predator is also affected by race. A white female typically has more power than a woman of color accusing a white male. Therefore, in a negotiation you must be aware of the dynamics that shape the negotiation and its flow.[12]

MANIPULATION

Harvey Weinstein was forced out of his studio and the Academy of Motion Picture Arts and Sciences. When the bully loses his power, observe what the other negotiator does. In theory, the person is powerless. Does he or she turn around to seek another source of power? Anticipate what people might do if you take their power base away.

For example, a wife felt she lost power when her husband stated his intention to seek a divorce. She then claimed she needed an extravagant amount of money to maintain her style of living. In this form of negotiation, the wife was using manipulative tactics to bully her husband.

Is this unusual? Everyone engaged in a negotiation is attempting to manipulate the other negotiator. By not assigning a label of good or bad to manipulation, we acknowledge that we all do it when we're negotiating. You want something from the negotiation; that is the reason you are negotiating.

An Internet service installer I met told me that he once made a quarter of a million dollars a year in a former executive position he held. Prior to when he and his wife divorced, if she wanted $100, he would give her $1,000. She was living like a queen before he lost that position. Then she started asking for more money. If she needed $100, she would ask for $2,000 instead. When he would probe to find out what she wanted to do with the money, it turned out to be something frivolous. He said that he could tell by her body language that she was making it up on the spot.

His strategy was, instead of looking for another high-paying job, he became an Internet service installer, earning substantially less than what he had been making. When she took him back to court to get more alimony, the judge awarded her less than she wanted because her ex-husband had a history of being generous with her. Always consider what the parties engaged in the negotiation have experienced in the past. To a degree, what occurred in the past will have a hand in shaping the outcome of the negotiation.

My motto is: You're always negotiating. Be concerned if someone tries to manipulate you. What you do today influences tomorrow's outcome.

OVERLY AGGRESSIVE BEHAVIOR

People displaying overly aggressive behavior are not always bullies. Some aggressive individuals may be in a heightened state of anger when they're trying to send a signal to someone else. The receiver of the message could say, "You're bullying me" and the person who sent the message could say, "That's not my intent." The receiver is reading the message one way and the sender is intending to send it a separate way. Thus, the two must reconcile how they're going to communicate.

What one should note afterward is the changes that come about as the result of the exchange. If the bully or the perceived bully softens his position with the words he uses and the body language he conveys, then he will have dispelled the perception he was bullying.

Here's why you must be careful when negotiating with a bully. Let's say the receiver simply stated, "I think you're bullying me" when the other person's behavior did not warrant that conclusion. That person is only using it to get the other negotiator to soften his language and his perspective as to how he engages in the negotiation. It could be nothing more than a ploy, so you should be attuned to it.

Suppose the sender of the message said, "My intent was not to bully you, nor was it to send a message of me trying to bully you, so I'm going to speak from this position. Understand it's not bullying. Are we in agreement?"

That shifts the dynamics in the negotiation at that point because of what the sender has communicated: "I'm going to continue speaking the same way. It's not intended as a bullying tactic. Can we go from here? I'm offering you some feedback so that I may consider altering my perspective later." This message shifts the perception of the other negotiator and enables a more cooperative spirit in the negotiation.

Some bullies may not consider themselves to be bullying somebody in a negotiation. Instead, they may consider themselves as overly aggressive or just negotiating. In some parts of the world it is commonplace to reject the first offer and to make a counter rebuttal. If you expected an offer of $500 and instead the person offered you $1,000, you might reject it simply because that is what is customary. You may do so in an aggressive style because that's the prevalent style in your environment. Know what is commonplace in the environment in which you are negotiating.

You might not consider this behavior to be bullying because you are accustomed to this tactic. If you're someone who is not accustomed to negotiating in such an aggressive style, to you it might be bullying.

The communication style can alter throughout the negotiation. When you negotiate with a bully, you might think, "He was aggressive before, but now he's screaming. We may have escalated this to the point we can now classify it as bullying." The way you perceive his actions will also dictate to a degree how you will respond to his actions. Be aware of the mind games going on in a negotiation and always try to maintain control to display the demeanor appropriate for that segment of the negotiation.

THE MOTIVATIONS OF BULLIES

In most cases, bullies want respect. They also want to be perceived as leaders so others will say, "Wow, she's a great leader. She knows how to get things done." They like accolades. You can look at people in political power as an example. If you want to be on their favorable side, all you need to do is to compliment them and they will melt in your hands. They like people who like them.

Your understanding of the bully's attributes helps you establish your negotiating strategy. When you dissect the factors that motivate him, you realize how to manipulate him to move into a direction that helps you seek a successful negotiation outcome. Ask yourself the following questions to help get you started.

- ▶ Does he want more power?
- ▶ What might he do to get it?
- ▶ If he wants more recognition, what does that really mean to him?
- ▶ Does he want to project a certain persona?
- ▶ Is it likeability that he's most after?
- ▶ Is it that he wants to be portrayed as a tough guy?

All of those elements are motivating factors that bullies may possess at times throughout a negotiation. Do your homework prior to entering a negotiation to understand more of those attributes. Seek to determine how he uses them, when he uses them, why he uses them, and what he wants to obtain as the result of using them.

The bully who wants recognition may be stimulated as a concession when he continues down the path. Each negotiation will depend on the situation; there is no one-size-fits-all.

The way you motivate somebody today can change tomorrow simply because of what has occurred in that twenty-four-hour period. Your insight drives you to determine whether or not you give her this win so she can show that she's doing something more positive. Knowing more about the mindset of bullies allows you to recognize what to give them, what to withhold from them, and when to do so. This may either enhance or detract from the negotiation.

When I say enhance, I'm speaking of increments. You can enhance the increments in a negotiation slightly or greatly depending on whether what you have at that time is life-saving versus life-ending. When someone truly needs a heart doctor because she's just had a heart attack she does not go into the information-gathering mode asking, "How much does this doctor cost? What other options might I exercise?" All she wants are relief of pain and medical attention.

Depending upon the situation that you're in, you can withhold or extend anything of perceived value to the other negotiator so that he or she will act.

BODY SIZE

Bullies come in all assorted sizes. Very small bullies and very large bullies can pose challenges. For example, a height disparity can influence bullying behavior. Let's look at a fictional scenario to help us envision what I mean:

Neurosurgeon Dr. Antonio Rizzo found Nurse Kindra Howard in the hallway. "I demand to know why my patient has not gotten out of bed yet. It is 2 p.m. and he should be up in the chair by now."

Kindra gazed down at 5'1" Dr. Rizzo. "Dr. Rizzo, your patient had to go through the CT scan you ordered."

"I don't care," Dr. Rizzo yelled. "He should be up in the chair. I want him up now! Do you hear me?"

"Yes, Doc," she murmured.

"And don't call me Doc. I am *Doctor* Rizzo."

As Kindra entered the nursing station, she muttered to the unit secretary, "Little Napoleon is at it again."

Beyond this encounter with the nurse, Dr. Rizzo also had temper tantrums in the operating room, where he threw instruments at the nurses and OR technicians. He demanded that the head nurse accompany him when he went on rounds even though she was busy with other priorities. Dr. Rizzo is a good example of a bully using his size as the catalyst for his behavior.

The Napoleon complex or short man syndrome is a theory that some short people are overly aggressive to compensate for their height. The Napoleon complex is named after Emperor Napoleon Bonaparte of France. He measured 5'7" at his death.[12] In the purported Napoleon complex, the short person is trying to act bigger than his physical size or image. (There is some debate about whether this theory is supported by research.) A bully whose mindset is affected by his short stature may be more harmful than an average-size person. His behavior is designed to tell others, "Don't underestimate me."

A large person may be perceived as a bully simply because of size. There may be an assumption the bully will use body size as a psychological weapon. Large people's defense mechanisms guide their behavior and can sometimes make them self-conscious of their height. A girl I grew up with got the nickname "Tree" because of her height. She walked stooped over so people could not see exactly how tall she was. A friend of mine who is 6'9" got tired of people always asking him as a kid, "How's the air up there?" He developed an attitude that conveyed, "You can approach me if you want, but don't come with high jokes because I don't play those games." In some cases, being short or tall may make people act like bullies.

Mind games enable you to take charge of a situation with a bully. You could be confrontational with him depending on how he reacts to you. That might be enough to subdue him; it may also be enough to make him challenge you more. You would need to determine the degree of confrontation to use. Going back to our fictional scenario, an operating room nurse might say to Dr. Rizzo, "You throw another retractor at me and I am out of this room and you will need to finish surgery by yourself." On the other hand, knowing the neurosurgeon had a Napoleon complex, you might instead choose to show him deference. "Good morning, Doctor Rizzo. How are you doing today? I am looking forward to helping you with this surgery."

Somewhere between these two boundaries is the right approach for the situation and bully. Keep in mind that most short people and large people are not bullies. The perception people have of themselves and the environment they are in will determine how that person reacts. You must understand not only how that person projects herself based on the way she sees herself, but you must take into consideration how she thinks others see her based on her size.

THE MAKING OF A BULLY

Although tempting, it is not possible to generalize what turns a person into a bully. I am always cautious about painting any subject matter with a broad brush. A person could have been bullied throughout his childhood but turn out to be the exact opposite of a bully. Or a person could have been bullied and turn out to be a bully because of being bullied.

Bullying can be caused by a host of factors to include a genuine lack of inherent empathy on the individual's behalf, emulation of bullying as seen in the household, feeling personally bullied, lack of control over emotions, or it could simply be attention-seeking behavior.[13]

When I was a kid, I was bullied. Because of this, I chose to increase my strength as I got older to combat that. My experiences also led me to become more compassionate about the needs and concerns of others.

Now, you can take the same situation that I encountered as a kid and contrast that with a bully who beats people up due to what he encountered when he was a kid. You need to know the individual and understand his real source of motivation. Suppose you make assumptions about the other negotiator—that he was bullied as a kid so he's going to bully you in this negotiation. If that is the case, what you have done is set a level of expectations that you're now basing your negotiation strategy upon. That could start you off from the wrong path with false assumptions about his behavior.

Bullying behaviors can be changed and does not need to persist throughout one's life. However, it does take a very hands-on approach. A conversation needs to take place that is very specific about the type of behaviors being displayed, the harmful effects to others, and alternative positive behavioral possibilities. Encourage other ways that the individual can be deemed popular or powerful. Also, taking a greater interest in the individual when he or she is not bullying is also a way of promoting prosocial behavior. Discussing the actual feelings being experienced by a bully is a good way to get to the root of the problem that is likely causing the bullying behavior.[14]

PRIMING

Priming is the preparation you undertake before a negotiation. Think of it like the primer you would use when you are about to paint something. The compound allows the paint to stick better and last longer. When it comes to priming as it relates to a negotiation, think about the mindset that you want to have in a negotiation and how you want to use that mindset with your strategies.

Depending on the value of the outcome of the negotiation, you can employ all kinds of strategies to gain insight about other individuals. We see that happening with some of our public associations and agencies in the federal government. They dig into the background information of individuals to find out their weak points. Once they identify the points of weakness, they know how they can manipulate that person during a negotiation.

Use some of the same techniques to gain more understanding about the other negotiator so you can help him see it's beneficial to work with you. Discover more about how that person came to possess his mindset so you can predict how he will behave during a negotiation with you.

The other negotiator may have grown up in an environment in which he believed himself to be superior based on his ethnicity or race. He comes into a negotiation with that type of mindset because as a kid that was what he was exposed to. If you understand that about him, you will adopt a strategy that is conducive to knowing he grew up in an alternative environment. Be prepared for it. Once he displays the attitude that says you're less capable than him, be prepared to do something to jolt him, such as stand up, shout, and bang the table. "You're not going to treat me like that. We can stop this negotiation right now unless you change your stance." Meanwhile you are pointing your finger in the air as though you were stabbing someone. That body language gesture adds strength to your statement. Those are the types of things you need to be prepared to implement.

Don't let that preparation put you in the mindset of just waiting for something to happen to utilize this strategy. That can put you into a very bad place mentally because all you're doing is sitting there waiting. The other negotiator happens to say something that triggers your expectations of his behavior and you're off and running. He's looking at you and thinking, "What is the matter with this maniac?" Be mindful of how you might utilize a strategy and don't let it be triggered needlessly.

Knowing what will motivate the person to move in one direction versus another gives you insight about how you're going to prime that person. In the case of the unpopular bully who is standing alone against the opinions of others, you might prime him by providing yourself as an ally. Priming is something that you use as a tool to enhance your negotiation effort based on the needs and wants of the other negotiator. You can always note the response to determine to what degree your priming efforts are working.

We can use an event with President Donald Trump as a good example of priming. When President Trump reached across the aisle to deal with the Democrats on an attempt at finding a political solution to a challenge, he was praised by both MSNBC, which leans to the left, and Fox News, which leans to the right.

The fact that President Trump wanted to be liked and wanted to receive positive press caused him to reach out. That reaction was a result of his priming efforts, as it sends the message that he responds to positive press. People who wanted to work with him would find other situations in which they could invoke a similar type of circumstance that would allow them to get the same type of response. This technique allows them to be in a more powerful position when they're negotiating with that individual.

One of the ways we train children is to give positive reinforcement when they do something correct. Positive reinforcement plays a huge role when negotiating, but there is a risk of being effusive. The bully thinks, "Here he goes again, throwing a number of compliments at me." Overusing positive reinforcement causes it to lose its effectiveness. Strike a balance, as it is only one of the many mind games we play while negotiating.

Let's look at the flipside of giving positive reinforcement. What happened in most cases when you were a kid and you came home with a grade that was not as good as your parents thought you could achieve? What usually occurred in that situation? In most cases the parents either chose to say nothing or something like "You can do better." Now, the parent may not know what went into the efforts to get that lower grade; you could have been working really hard to improve in that subject matter. Maybe the grade was reflective of your capability or maybe it wasn't, but what happens to the positive reinforcement at that time?

The same thing occurs in a negotiation. A bully may think he did exceptionally well to grant you the concessions you needed. He had to go back to his boss to get approval. Meanwhile, you're thinking your efforts resulted in the concessions. The bully does not get the level of recognition he feels he deserves.

When it comes to positive reinforcement be very careful of how you use it and when you use it. If it's given too much it loses its effectiveness. If it's missing or not delivered to the degree it should be (as perceived by the person receiving the positive reinforcement) it doesn't have the same level of impact. Use it sparingly.

ROLE-PLAYING AS PREPARATION

The degree of practice in which you engage before an important negotiation is determined by the severity of the negotiation. If you are going to enter a negotiation for small stakes, it's not as important to role-play. Nevertheless, when you are negotiating for something on a larger scale, you should engage in a role-play situation so that you understand more of the nuances of what might occur in the negotiation. In so doing, you will be able to negotiate a whole lot better.

In any negotiation you should practice to the degree the negotiation outcome is important to your overall plan. That strategy becomes magnified when you know in advance that you're negotiating with a bully. A bully does *not* say to himself, "I'll go along to get along. I'll trust you to a degree that I can see where it is no longer beneficial for me to trust you."

The bully has a completely different thought process that says, "I'm going to do something to you because I need some form of self-gratification." Therefore, it becomes more important to role-play before negotiating with a bully because you need to understand the aspect from which you may have to negotiate with that bully. Think about the following questions to help you prepare for such a situation.

► Will he bully you to a point that requires you to show you have forces to make him bend to your wishes? What might those forces look like?

► How long might it take you to assemble such forces and to what degree will those forces be relevant based on his counter measures?

► What tactics are you going to use if you need to gather support?

► What might the bully do in return to offset whatever forces you throw up to combat him?

▶ How long might it take him to go about assembling such forces?

▶ What occurs if the bully backs down?

▶ Will the bully undertake behind-the-back tactics to get even with you later?

These are things that you can uncover when you role-play before negotiating with a bully, which is why it is so advantageous to do so. Depending on the emotional state of mind the bully maintains or is forced into you must take into consideration to what degree he might be belligerent or violent.

Some bullies will use intimidation tactics to sway you to appreciate their power and to recognize their power. For example, during the 2016 presidential campaign there was one candidate who stood behind the other candidate while she was speaking. The perceived bully was projecting the message, "I'm watching over you. I'm standing behind you, so I may do something behind your back." It was an attempt at intimidation. When you are engaged with a bully, he may engage in things that, had you not role-played, you would not have expected.

And by the way, that former presidential candidate eventually disclosed that she felt shaken by the fact that he was lurking behind her. His demeanor personified his misogynistic attitude. This presidential male candidate was viewed as being irrational.

The female candidate had prepared for the debates by doing role-play situations, but had not anticipated the other candidate would be lurking behind her. Because she was not prepared for this, she was somewhat jarred by his actions.

The ideal person to role-play with prior to a negotiation is someone who is most like the person or team you will be negotiating against. For example, a boxer practices for an upcoming fight with someone who has the same characteristics of the person he will be fighting. If his opponent is going to be left-handed, he will have sparring partners who are left-handed. The same thing is true when it comes to role-playing and how you're going to engage in the role-play against an opponent and his team.

Take into consideration what a bully's team might look like. Are they individuals like him? To what degree are they like him? To what degree is the bully the front person responsible for uncovering your tactics (if it's a team negotiation environment)?

You would have to create multiple tactics if you're negotiating with an individual who is a bully versus if you're negotiating with an entity who happens to be on a team of bullies. If you're negotiating with a team of bullies, use your role-playing to consider what type of wedge issues you might use. Wedge issues are used to cause the opposing team to separate so that you get them to fight among one another.

When you think about how to use these strategies, you need to understand exactly what type of mindset you're going to be negotiating against. You need to anticipate what your tactics might do as far as how they may cause the opposing negotiation team to react. You can include as many situations in your role-play strategies as possible and as a result you can then become better prepared to address any negotiation situation you are confronted with. This will allow you to negotiate more effectively.

Select a practice partner based on the type of bully you expect to confront. Suppose there is a softcore bully involved (a person who is just testing the waters). Consider that he's going to try to create a blustering image of himself just to see to what degree you allow him to have his way with you.

The hardcore bully feels as though he has resources to sustain his tactics as you challenge him. Once you challenge him, he may back down (as would be the case of the softcore bully), but the hardcore bully may take a lot longer to do so.

When you are negotiating with a softcore bully versus a hardcore bully there are supporting tactics you can employ. Sometimes you can simply act irrational, which backs a bully down or at least causes the bully to expose his hand so you know more of his real plans.

If you negotiate too stringently against a softcore bully, you can harden him. On the contrary, you can make the hardcore bully even more strident in his attempts to show or prove his worth if you negotiate too harshly against him. In your role-playing situations, you need to consider the degree to which you are going to confront hardcore or soft-core bullies and how your confrontation may cause them to alter their position.

You need to test multiple strategies when role-playing. Anticipate what the bully may do in response to the positions you take. For every action there's a reaction, and you need to be as well prepared for every contingency you might encounter when you're in a tense negotiation with a bully.

The Internet can be a useful resource when it comes to role-playing strategies. You can find a person to participate in a role-play as well as look for negotiation resources and ideas for how to assemble a team. You can also look at some historical perspectives about negotiating with tyrants or bullies and who was on the teams. Information gathering is a crucial step in any negotiation or role-playing situation, and to do so effectively sets up your role-play situation for a positive outcome.

Include both softcore and hardcore bullies during your role-playing experiences. For example, if you map out a negotiation strategy that causes a hardcore bully to soften, you would have someone on your team role-play a bully who was originally hardcore but became a lot softer or vice-versa.

That's why, depending upon the outcome you seek and the value proposition, you should have as many characteristics of bullies within the negotiation team and the role-playing team as possible.

- ▶ Does the hardcore bully go to softcore?
- ▶ Does the softcore go to hardcore?
- ▶ Do they transform into middlecore bullies?
- ▶ How do they get there?
- ▶ What strategies caused them to get there?
- ▶ What strategy did you adopt that caused them to carry out different strategies other than what you projected might be the case?

These thoughts go into the makeup of the strategy you will use in your role-playing situation to negotiate with a bully. You will be better prepared when you can simulate as many aspects of the bully's perspective as you can. The role-playing experience foreshadows the dynamics of engaging with the hardcore, softcore, and middlecore bullies.

The person (actor) who plays the part of the bully should be skilled in human dynamics, be able to think like a bully, and predict how a bully would respond to negotiation tactics. The actor can prepare for the roleplay by reading books on bullying and getting training at a negotiation association. These organizations have negotiators on staff. The actor might ask, "If I were to be negotiating in a particular situation, what type of negotiators would you suggest I use to help me prepare for a role-play?" It is relatively easy to find the correct role-playing techniques if you reach out to negotiation associations. (My other book, *Body Language Secrets to Win More Negotiations,* gives details on how you can become more astute when it comes to negotiating in different psychological environments.) Role-playing with a person who has a background in psychology could be advantageous because of the deeper understanding of human behavior and what to expect from a bully during a negotiation.

THE PERCEPTION OF BULLYING IN NEGOTIATIONS

The concept of bullying during a negotiation is subjective. One person who might be labeled a bully may not think of himself in that light because he is unaware he's being perceived as bullying others. When I oversaw a team of speakers, we were due to have reports in at a certain time. There was one individual who constantly missed the due date. Finally, I wrote a message to that person: "Here is the team's report. It's missing your report again. We'll work more diligently on this as we go forward."

I received a response back from the person accusing me of being passive-aggressive. I thought to myself, "Boy, compared to what I wanted to say, my message was toned down." The perception of bullying depends on the people involved in the negotiation. You must call it what it is if you think it's affecting the negotiation and it is necessary to confront the bully. When I say "confront," I mean you can pose a question to that individual, such as, "Can you tell me what's happening right now?" If you ask an open-ended question in that manner the person may ask, "What do you mean?" That gives you the opportunity to gather more information about person's thought process.

Identification of bullying starts with discerning the other negotiator's normal style of negotiating. Is he the type of person who will give and take and then suddenly become much more aggressive? Before you term that as bullying, understand why that person became more aggressive. Gain insight by asking the person, "Something has changed. You seem to be a little more aggressive. What is going on?" Word choice matters here also. "You seem to be a little more aggressive" is more likely to start a discussion than labeling the behavior as "You're bullying me."

If you assert "You're bullying me" you might instigate a defensive reaction: "No, I'm not bullying you." Consider what might happen if you turned this around to a question: "Are you bullying me right now?" That question allows the other negotiator to pause to reflect on the negotiation.

If the person answers the first question ("What is going on?") with "I'm being a little aggressive right now," it signals that he is aware of his tactics.

To summarize, whether or not somebody is bullying you or to what degree he may be bullying you is dependent upon the people who are involved in the negotiation. To what degree you wish to raise the issue is determined by how you feel about where the negotiation is headed. There's a difference between the perception of aggressiveness and bullying in the mind of some people when they are negotiating. Based on culture or ethnicity, that style can be interpreted or misinterpreted.

Suppose you ask, "Are you bullying me?" and the person says, "Oh no. I'm sorry, that's not my intent at all." You may see a milder behavior after that because he is now concerned about not being perceived as a bully. That's invaluable information in a negotiation. Talk about manipulation! You can then use that insight to push that other negotiator's buttons. He doesn't want to be perceived as a bully, so all you have to do is play the meek and timid role of somebody being bullied and then call him on it. The next thing you know he's backing down again. Do that strategically when you want a concession you know you would have a challenge getting.

Observe how the other negotiator uses tactics that approach or move away from bullying. Think about how you will utilize this feedback as you go through the negotiation process. You should be aware of it because it is invaluable insight you can utilize throughout the negotiation. Being aware of it will also lend insight to where you are in the negotiation based on the role-playing you engaged in.

When you're embarking upon a negotiation with somebody whom you don't know, you might not have any idea that the person's behavior is going to turn into bullying. In other situations, perhaps in a business situation where you're routinely working with people, you may know one of your colleague's negotiation style turns into a bullying behavior when confronted with opposition or not getting what he wants. In the situation where you have identified the person ahead of time who typically acts like a bully in a business environment, it is important to understand that bully's mindset before you negotiate with him. Depending upon how valuable the outcome of that negotiation is, you should know as much about that person as you possibly can.

Let's say you are starting a negotiation without knowing a whole lot about the person's mindset. As you begin the negotiation try to observe certain clues. To what degree is the person friendly? To what degree is the person somewhat aggressive?

Note when his demeanor changes and what caused it to do so. Also assess to what degree the change is feigned or real to get insight into the direction that he might attempt to take the negotiation in.

Based on your perception you can then test those conclusions by asking certain questions to determine what the person is really seeking from this negotiation. If he says, "I need to get it done as quickly as possible" you know time is important to him. As time passes and you observe him becoming a little more aggressive, you know the source of that aggressiveness is due to the time constraints he feels. Understand the motivation for what's causing him to act that way.

Let's look at it from the other side. This person is being over-aggressive with you initially and that morphs into him bullying you, but you're oblivious to it. What is he thinking? He's getting more upset as you're responding to his offers because you don't feel as though you're being bullied and he's attempting to do so. He takes his bullying efforts to a higher level and he continues to do that until he gets some type of recognition from you.

His mindset causes him to do what he does. This helps you anticipate some of his actions so that you can be better prepared. You also need to understand other sources of motivation that are causing him to engage in the negotiation. Suppose his boss said, "You let that last negotiator get away with too much. I expect you to become a little stronger when it comes to negotiating with outside vendors." Now this guy has entered your negotiation with these thoughts and that mindset: "I'm going to get my way to show my superior that I'm a better negotiator than he thinks I am." That mindset is going to generate different actions than if his superior said, "It seems like you browbeat the supplier in this last negotiation. This could come back to bite the company. Maybe you should back off a little bit."

You need to understand his mindset at the onset of the negotiation, what causes him to alter his perspective, and to what degree you can manipulate him to see things from your point of view.

MANIPULATION AND BACK-DOOR STRATEGEIS

When you're in a negotiation, time can be your ally, especially if you know the other negotiator is pressured by time. You can alter his behavior by slowing the pace of the negotiation down or go as far as using silence to stall.

You can also alter the pace of the negotiation with the speed at which you speak. When things are going badly and he's under a time constraint, you start to speak slower. When things are going well, you speak a little faster. Voice inflection is a way to alter his perspective.

In addition to time, the body language of looking down your nose conveys you are skeptical about what he said. Casting doubt about the believability of what he's saying is another way to alter his perspective. Clearing your throat also conveys doubt. The nonverbal message is "That's clogging me up." Getting up from the table if you're face to face in a negotiation or walking around as though you have a pain in the neck are yet other ways to use your body language to convey a non-verbal message.

Now suppose you reach an impasse and the other negotiator is trying to bully you. You have confronted the negotiator about his bullying tactics but he continues or even escalates his bullying efforts. You can be direct by saying, "If you want this negotiation to proceed according to our plans, this is what I need from you. I expect to see a change in your behavior. Now do we continue or do we stop?" This is an exit point that allows you to define the end of the negotiation.

It's always good to realize that you have a certain amount of time to allocate toward this negotiation. When you don't have limits on time, the more time you psychologically invest in the negotiation the more you will want to see the conclusion of the negotiation. As you get closer to what you perceive to be the end of the negotiation you might start making concessions you would not normally make had you not invested so much time.

A "back door" in a negotiation is a strategy to escape. Depending on the strategy you plan to use, you can leave that back door slightly cracked. "I can tell that we're not going to reach a successful outcome today. How about if we reconvene next week?" That's also part of your exit point planning as you prepare for the negotiation.

The back-door strategy can also be something long term. "I can tell right now that something seems to be troubling you. I'm not exactly sure what it is, but you seem to be participating in what I would term bullying tactics. I can't deal with that. Do you have a suggestion as to how we can overcome this?" In asking someone else for a suggestion on how to address a problem, you get insight into how she views the problem and how she might go about solving the problem. That can become part of your back-door strategy when you reach an impasse in the negotiation.

If you understand how she is viewing the problem and her ideas for a solution, you have now gotten more insight about the methods you can use to address the problem.

However, you might not want to address it fully because if the person is experiencing some form of discomfort but you know he wants to stay engaged in the negotiation, you can let him sweat. That's part of your back-door strategy to bring him back into the fold.

To summarize, the back-door strategy can be used to exit the negotiation, to offset a potential impasse in the negotiation, or to stop a negotiation and reengage at another point. It's a strategy that serves as an off-ramp to exit the negotiation.

Urgency affects negotiations; something may be taken away if the negotiation with a bully is not concluded by a specific point. Using the tool of urgency is based on knowing what will motivate that bully. Consider creating urgency by saying this deal is offered until whatever time frame you cite. Don't weaken your negotiation position by extending the deadline if the other negotiator does not do follow through in time. Be cautious about using a sense of urgency in a negotiation, however. If you say something such as, "Get it today; tomorrow it's gone!" is it really gone tomorrow? Now what do you do? If you only have 30 days to negotiate, what will you do on day 31?

A bully may be testing you by not abiding to your deadline. Bullies will use tactics of scarcity or deadlines to apply more pressure in a negotiation. Be aware of the mind games when you're negotiating so that you don't fall prey to such pressures. If you're the one who is issuing edicts about urgent deadlines, make sure what you say is appropriate about what you're offering.

You can also position such offerings as, "If you do this by this time, you will get XYZ." This creates a softer spot from which to exit the negotiation. The bully realizes "He said it's only available until this date. The fact that he was willing to offer it means that if I do the right thing at the right time I can get what I want."

In Conclusion

The more you understand the bully's mindset, the better you can negotiate with that person. You should know to what degree that person may become irrational, what that person's trigger points are, and what he's going to do if he cannot negotiate satisfactorily with you. You should also consider that there might be someone not visible at the negotiation table who is driving the agenda and directing the actions of the bully.

If you understand more pieces of her mental puzzle as you go about negotiating with her, you will be able to assemble a more brilliant vibrant picture of a negotiation outcome: one that serves both her and you.

I have additional resources regarding this topic on my website *http:// themasternegotiator.com/negotiating-with-a-bully.*

Homework

Observe your personal and work environment to identify a bully. If you have no firsthand exposure to a bully, watch TV or movies to identify examples of bullies. Determine the type of bully: hardcore, middlecore, or softcore.

By gaining more insight into bullying styles and the source that motivates that style of negotiator, you will be better prepared to identify the type of bully you will be dealing with before you enter a negotiation.

2

Body Language: Interpreting the Signals

The first thing Sean noticed when he entered the conference room was Jayla standing in the corner of the room. With her hands on her hips, she loudly told Pierre, "We will *not* accept the terms of that client! There is no reason for us to modify our agreement. They need us, and they know it." Jayla shook her finger in Pierre's face as she made her points. "I will not tolerate being jerked around. It is time to remind them of how desperately they need our services and we will not deviate from our agreement."

Sean realized how upset Jayla was as he watched the conversation. "I would hate to be on the receiving end of that temper," he thought. "I wonder if Jayla is ready to lose this client."

Body language reveals the mindset of the bully. Jayla conveyed her anger by putting her hands on her hips and shaking her finger. Knowing how to decode the bully's body language gives you an advantage in a negotiation. Body language plays an enormous role in the way bullies act. Here are a few elements to observe that can help you gain an advantage.

The Face

A bully's face is a window into his emotions. Focus on the bully's eyes. When the bully's eyes are directed at you, it is a sign he is becoming more alert to what you are saying or doing. Observe when the bully's pupils dilate. Take notice if you're close enough as to when the bully's eyes change. Dilated pupils allow the bully to take in more of his environment, explore more options, or perform some other type of action.

Does he break eye contact? Is he thinking about what will happen if he continues his behavior? Does he hesitate? Is there a pattern as to how he moves his eyes? For example, if he looks up to the left, he may be thinking of the past. "This guy has always behaved like a wimp. Why is he trying to push back now?" If he looks up and to the right he may be thinking, "Okay, what do I do now?" In addition, rubbing his ear indicates "I don't like what I'm hearing."

Watch his nostrils. When they start to flare, that means the person is trying to get more oxygen into his body simply because he's feeling more aggressive.

Carefully look at his facial features, especially his lips. To what degree are his lips spread, turned up, or turned down? Is he frowning, smiling, or scowling? If he has a frown on his face, he may be testing you by sending a message: "I don't like that you won't let me do what I'm attempting to do or what I want you to think I want to do with you." You may have heard the saying, "A smile is a frown turned upside down." If he truly has a frown on his face he's moving more toward an aggressive state. His smile may mean, "I'm testing you to see exactly how far you will let me go." Watch for the appearance of a scowl in relation to a frown or a smile. A scowl may balance between the two positions.

Observe how the bully uses facial expressions to make you cower. Does she grimace when making threatening gestures? If so, that might indicate she is doing so half-heartedly. Such a display may lead you to conclude that she is testing you to see how far she can go before you push back.

Consider this situation: An expert witness was being cross-examined by the opposing attorney during a trial. The attorney was trying to get the expert to make concessions that would help his case, but the expert kept holding firm to the points she was making. The attorney turned beet red. The expert could almost see the steam coming out of his ears. The attorney finally sat down, totally frustrated, because she was winning all the points. The attorney who hired the expert won the case.

Any lawyer, like in any negotiation, should have some idea of the answer before asking the question. Anticipating the answer will help the attorney plan alternate strategies if the answer is something other than what he expected to hear.

A popular concept among many professions, lawyers included, is "You should never ask a question you don't know the answer to." It's the same thing when you're presenting such a scenario to a bully. You want to know what your efforts are going to do. Skin colorization change is one clue something is happening in the bully's mind. When it comes to body language, the body never attempts to lie on purpose and will do things to stay in a state of comfort. When the body experiences discomfort it manifests into certain body language, such as blood rushing to the lawyer's face, which caused him to become beet red. Depending upon the race of the bully, you can see a person's pigmentation changing if you closely observe them.

Flushing occurs as the person turns red because the person is filled with emotion. The increasing blood flow may be evident either on the bully's face or on the target's face. From a body language perspective, the target's flushing is a reaction that could come from a realization of the seriousness of the situation.

When you first see the bully's red flush beginning, you know it was the statement you made that caused the person to react. From a negotiation perspective, it means you might be able to force the person to back down. Or the flush may be a warning sign that the person is going to lose emotional control. Either way, it is a warning sign that something is occurring in that person's thought process.

Be especially observant of other body language at the time you see the flushing. Let's say the person clenched his fist, turned red, and took one step forward with one foot. He's now getting into a stance where he could be ready to start fighting.

In another scenario, suppose the person flushes and takes two steps back from you. You see her hands are open and she's wiggling her fingers, which could be an indication that she's trying to soothe herself. "Comfort gestures" mean a person needs to reassure herself everything is okay, but it is also more likely she is mentally and physically backing away from you. She wants to get away from the situation. At the negotiation table, let that person escape to save face.

Consider this tactic during a negotiation with a bully when you see him flushing: "You can see the nasty side of me or you can see the good side of me. Which side would you prefer to deal with in a negotiation?"

I covered micro-expressions in my book *Body Language Secrets to Win More Negotiations*. They are expressions that last less than one second but give you a true snapshot of another person's mindset. Micro-expressions can include:

▶ Eyes widening to take in more of the environment, which indicates interest, alertness, surprise, shock, or dismay.

▶ An increase in breathing rate, which means he is experiencing emotion, such as anger, before becoming aggressive.

▶ Fear shown by the eyebrows raised and together.

▶ Disgust shown by her raised upper lip and wrinkled nose (like smelling something foul).

▶ Surprise shown with widened eyes, raised eyebrows, and an opened mouth.

▶ Contempt shown by raising a corner of the lip.

▶ Sadness shown by turning down the corners of the mouth, drooping eyelids, and losing eye focus.

▶ Happiness shown when she elevates her cheeks and you see stretch marks around the eyes.

Throat

Watch the bully's throat to see if he starts swallowing. If so, he's indicating that he's getting a little more nervous. If you sense he's feeling uncomfortable, you can do one of two things: You can alter the pace of the negotiation by speaking more slowly, which is an attempt to decrease the emotion you may both be feeling. Or you can point out the fact you don't feel as ready to engage in a negotiation giving the current environment. That would more than likely force him to ask, "Why are you saying that?" You could respond, "I'm sensing this negotiation is getting a little tense." By drawing attention to the emotion, you may be able to decrease the emotional tone of the conversation.

Rubbing the neck may have significance as well. The expression "You're a pain in my neck" actually has some truth to it when you're negotiating. Something creates consternation or presents a challenge and you then see the person rubbing his neck. He could be thinking, "What else does he want from me? I've given him everything he's asked for. This is getting a bit painful."

Hands

In addition to watching the bully's face, pay attention to her hands. Are her hands reaching toward you? If so, she's indicating she's going to do something to you.

Is she clenching her fingers into a fist? She may be ready to strike. Is she keeping her hands close to her side? She may be feeling defensive according to what she's saying to you, but that gesture could indicate she's getting ready to hit you. Note how she positions her body in relation to yours. If you want to be forceful when hitting someone, you must start as close to your body as you can to land a powerful blow.

Clapping may mean the person is also getting ready for an aggressive act. If he starts to do so rapidly, that's a good sign that he's getting ready to go into battle and he's going to do so very shortly.

Flushing may show up on the bully's hands, which is a warning sign as well. The more you pay attention to small physical changes such as these, the more astute you will be in gaining insight as to whether it's time to back away or charge forward.

The way the bully shakes your hand may also convey significant messages. If your hand and a bully's hand are shaking parallel to one another, both individuals are indicating they are equal. However, in a parallel handshake, the person who releases the handshake last is the person who's really in control of the negotiation. If I'm holding your hand in a handshake, I'm controlling you. I decide when to let you go because I'm in control.

If you have one hand on top of the other in a handshake, the hand on top of the other one is saying, "I'm on top of you. I'm the person in the power position. I recognize it and I'm going to control you." The position of the person's hand on the bottom says, "I'm being submissive. Do with me as you wish. I will be your puppet if that's what you want me to be."

There are bullying techniques that can be projected into the handshake of two individuals before and during a negotiation. One way to test someone's demeanor after a negotiation has reached an impasse is to say, "It seems like this discussion is going nowhere." Get up, extend your hand to shake the other person's hand, and note any differences that have occurred from the initial handshake. Handshakes send very subliminal nonverbal messages about how someone feels at a moment in time. It is a small signal that always has value in a negotiation.

A great example of the impact of a handshake is President Trump. Upon meeting Vladimir Putin, President Trump allowed his hand to be on the bottom during the initial handshake. The reason that was so noteworthy is because it feeds into the theory that there's something causing President Trump to act submissive when it comes to the Russians. This reinforces the need to observe the bully's body language in different environments, which will add insight as to why he acts in a specific way.

As Robert C. Bordone wrote,

> To those of us who teach problem-solving negotiation, Trump perfectly embodies the techniques and stances we do *not* advocate. His behavior suggests that negotiations are always

played out on win/lose terms; that the party who prevails does so by smiting or crushing the other; that any effort to make an agreement a good deal for the other party is "weak" negotiating. Treating the other with respect and dignity and trying to forge an agreement that works for them (instead of one that just coerces them) is derided as "politically correct."[1]

TORSO

Observe the bully's face and hands but don't ignore how he positions his body. How closely aligned is his torso to yours? If it is directly facing you head-on, that's a more aggressive stance than if he's sideways. If he's turning sideways, he's indicating "I'm taking a glancing view of the situation and I'm not ready to confront you head on."

Suppose the bully rubs his stomach. He's indicating "Kinesthetically, I'm not feeling right about this."

FEET

The bully's feet also reveal his state of mind. Are his feet aligned with yours? If so, that sends the message of "I'm really focusing on you" more than if he had one foot pointed in a different direction than your feet.

The aggressive bully will more likely position his feet so he can hit you harder if he is getting ready to strike you. If someone is standing in front of you, it's harder to hit you than if he is placing his weight on his back foot. When the bully's feet are aligned with yours as he is making threatening gestures, he will be displaying a stronger commitment to his actions.

In addition, watch for the instance when the bully takes a step toward you. Does the bully step closer to you when making threatening gestures? He may be indicating he feels comfortable invading your personal space. Be alert to that gesture. If you take a step back, you allow the bully to take up your space. If that's the case, you're giving the bully a green light to be more aggressive, as opposed to you leaning into the bully. Don't step back. If you really wish to display a lack of fear, move closer to him. That will signal not only are you not afraid, but you are also willing to give back to him what he is attempting to give to you.

Conversely, if one or both of his feet are pointing away from you, that position indicates he is ready to escape the environment at the earliest opportunity. Give him an effortless way to exit the environment if you wish to rid yourself of him. Never say or do anything that would cause him to lose face or back him into a corner. An embarrassed and cornered bully can become very unpredictable. Verbal and physical violence may follow.

CONGRUENT BODY LANGUAGE

Observe if the person's body language is congruent with his words. For example, the bully says as he's covering his mouth, "I'm going to kick your butt." The bully is displaying through the action of having his hand over his mouth that he's holding those words back. He wants to soften the harshness of his words. It could also mean either "I don't like what someone is saying" or "I don't believe what I'm saying."

If the bully says, "I'm going to kick your butt" and he laughs, you should be alert. Ask yourself, "Is this guy serious about becoming more aggressive or does he want me to think he is?"

When North Korea launched one of its missile tests, President Trump said something to the effect that North Korea was playing with fire. The president said North Korea would incur all the consequences without anything being held back; they'd feel the full power and strength of the United States. However, the president's body language contradicted his message. He made this announcement while he had his arms folded around himself. That body language gesture was not consistent with his words. Suppose his hands were open and he was patting himself on his thighs. That would indicate he was trying to soothe himself as he was talking. Had he instead been stabbing with his pointed finger toward the desk at which he was sitting and making those same pronouncements, that would have implied a forceful demeanor and more conviction.

By him not displaying those stronger gestures he sent a signal that said something to the effect of, "I may be a paper tiger in this situation."

Let's say the leader of North Korea is also a bully. That nonverbal signal said, "We can test him again." Several weeks after President Trump made the announcement North Korea launched another missile. This escalated the situation.

Here's something else that occurred throughout the exchanges. North Korea's leader stated he would fire a test missile over Guam. In a stark address to the United Nations that raised the specter of nuclear warfare, President Trump threatened to "totally destroy" North Korea if the United States is forced to defend itself or its allies in East Asia. "Rocket Man is on a suicide mission for himself and for his regime," Trump told the 193-member U.N. General Assembly, using a mocking nickname for North Korea's leader, Kim Jong Un. Denouncing Pyongyang's "reckless" pursuit of nuclear weapons and ballistic missiles, Trump warned he would be prepared to take military action. "The United States has great strength and patience, but if it is forced to defend itself or its allies, we will have no choice but to totally destroy North Korea."[2]

ANTICIPATING BODY LANGUAGE

Here's the overarching point to keep in mind when you're engaged with a bully: You should know before even entering a negotiation with him what his demeanor might be in certain situations. Anticipate the type of body language he will display and how you're going to react. Suppose you know based on past negotiations that he is aggressive in the beginning. He takes this position to test the other negotiator. He leans in toward that person and tells him what to do: "If you don't do this deal with me I'll make sure I ruin you." You know his opening style of negotiation. You would lean right back into him and say, "Bring it on. I don't care. Who do you think you're talking to?" He is more likely to back down, depending upon his style of negotiation.

Your other choice is to act meek. You say, "Let me see if we can do business. Tell me what you have in mind." If you use a softer tone the bully may think, "I have this person exactly where I want him." As a result, the bully displays his negotiation plans and you now have greater insight as to how to deal with him. Be sure you match the type of body language the bully either thinks he's going to receive from you or the opposite based on the strategy you planned for how you're going to use your body language to combat him.

You may deliberately appear weak just to see what someone will do with the next phase of the negotiation. The response to you will be based on the perception of your strength or weakness. Sometimes weakness is nothing more than hidden strength disguised as weakness.

DECODING BODY LANGUAGE AT THE BEGINNING OF THE NEGOTIATION

- ▶ Be particularly observant of the body language a known bully displays at the beginning of your negotiation.
- ▶ Does he smile amiably at the beginning of the negotiation or before you get underway with the negotiation process?
- ▶ To what degree does he change his demeanor afterward?
- ▶ Exactly what body language does he use to project his bullying tactics and image?
- ▶ Does he say things that are just contrary?
- ▶ Does he outright lie?
- ▶ Does he lose eye contact as you hear him lie?

Bullying tactics come in many different forms. Observe how the bully displays himself in one manner and then changes as you engage in the beginning phases of the negotiation. If there is a change in his behavior, he's either doing so based on his plan or what *you* have done to influence the change.

SIZE MATTERS

Body size plays a key role in the body language signals that you adopt. Someone who is smaller than a bully who is standing in the bully's space could be trying to send the signal that the bully's size does not frighten the smaller person. When I was a kid, I was bullied a lot. Bigger kids used to take my money because I was a small kid. As a result, I learned to do two things well: One was to talk my way out of situations. When I couldn't I learned to run. Those were the tools I had at that age. I also realized that instead of running, I could build my body up so I appeared to be more intimidating. Therefore, a bully would not think to pick on me.

A smaller corporation could be figuratively standing in the larger corporation's space, facing a challenge. For example, Walmart has driven many small mom-and-pop shops out of existence because of their inability to provide the same range of products. Walmart also maintains a tight rein on its vendors through what it pays them. It uses its size and dominance to control those who want to do business with Walmart.

We love the underdog. The smaller corporation can elicit empathy from others because of the larger corporation's bullying: "What's it going to look like if you try to pick on me, you big giant?" The smaller business can use the empathy of others to create leverage to use against the bigger entity.

Size must be taken into consideration. The bigger company or person needs to evaluate the danger posed by the smaller entity's intention to not back down by asking, "Is there more to this than meets the eye?" The way you position yourself, the stance you adopt, and how you project your image play a significant role in any negotiation. Seek to offset his power if he's bigger than you. That is, have greater resources so he cannot use those resources in his effort to negotiate with you. You should be seeking such an advantage in most cases when you're dealing with a bully. The better prepared you are to implement your strategy to force a bully to back down the better your negotiation efforts will flow.

BODY LANGUAGE SIGNALS TO JUDGE EFFECTIVENESS OF NEGOTIATION

You need to know when you have won a negotiation. For instance, you sense the bully has been put in his place and he's making concessions. You think, "I never figured he would go for that." You push him a little further and he makes the next concession you ask for. Suddenly, he slams the palms of his hands on the table, exclaiming, "Enough already!" That's a very strong signal it may be time to back away from the bully.

This body language is a micro-expression, which means it is an expression that occurred in less than a second and that was unfiltered by the mind. The bully didn't think about slamming his hands down. He did so because he was at a point of frustration with having given in to you.

Let's say the bully has been smiling all along as you've been making one request after another. You've missed the cues. You just kept making one request after another without pausing to let him say yes or no to your request. That smile should capture your attention. You're not letting him speak, and there will be consequences.

If you miss that signal, you can get to the end of your request. Let's say it's a list of ten items you want him to agree to. He says with a sly smile on his face, "Is that all?" You reply, "No and I would like to have…" and you start rattling off even more demands. When you get to the end of it, he says, "Thank you very much. My answer is no." By missing the smile on his face, you ran a stop sign; you ran a signal that indicated, "Wait a minute, I better get some buy-in before I start putting the rest of my cards on the table because if I don't I'm actually hurting my negotiation efforts."

Observe for little signals like crossed arms at a time when you make a request. Or the bully places his hands down on the table as opposed to palms up on the table. Hands spread apart could indicate he's open as opposed to closed with him wrapping his arms around himself. If he stands up, he could be indicating he has had enough or needs a break.

All of those can be body language signs it's time, if not to back down, then at least to alter your perspective about what is being discussed. Ask yourself:

- ▶ "Why are we on this topic?"
- ▶ "What progress are we making?"
- ▶ "Why did he use that body language gesture?"

Take note of what he was conveying with that gesture, so you can gain insight about his thoughts and reactions.

If you take note of those signals you will have clues into not only his mindset, but the way he's thinking. By watching when each of those gestures occur, you'll have a better understanding of the progress of the negotiation.

There is another verbal signal you should note: to what degree he over talks you. For example, you feel a little intimidated about his proximity to you and decide to draw attention to it: "Wait a minute. I'm feeling a bit uncomfortable right now because you're a little too close to me physically." As you're saying those words, he says, "Oh no, don't worry about that." In this situation, the physical proximity can be akin to a car salesman moving closer to you while you are saying you are not happy with the current offer. As you make your opinion known, the salesman over talks you by saying, "Don't worry about anything. I'll take great care of you." The fact that he dismissed your position and did so by over talking you is a sign he doesn't have a high degree of respect for you and he's more interested in making the sale. The point is: You should be aware of both verbal and nonverbal signals. They will give you insight about what someone feels is most important in a situation.

Should you draw attention to the body language of the bully? The answer depends on the outcome you want from the negotiation. If you do not want him to be aware that you're taking notice of his body language gestures, there are certain signs you should not say anything about, such as swallowing or word choices he may be using. Consider the idea that some bullies may be astute at projecting body language signals and could be using them as a ploy.

OBSERVING FOR ESCALATION

Earlier in the chapter I detailed the body language that indicates an increase in aggression. If the bully is standing 15 feet from you and he's performing those gestures, you know you have more time before he erupts in anger. The intensity is very different if he is standing a few inches from you and doing the same thing. His proximity to you indicates he is trying to get you to back down or position himself so he can hit you. Take his body language into account before you determine to what degree his aggressiveness is accelerating.

A bully may not overtly display anger. This person approaches a negotiation with a steely determination to get his way, consistently asserts his demands, and is unwilling to negotiate. He uses power techniques to manipulate you. They will have less impact if you are negotiating over the phone or through email.

One bullying tactic may be nothing more than silence in response to your negotiation point. That says, "I'll leave you to play with yourself in your own head." That could be a form of mental bullying.

Another nonverbal signal you can observe is to what degree the pace of the conversation has changed even if you're face to face. Has the person started to slow down or speed up his responses? Does the person use threatening gestures even if he's saying nonthreatening words?

Look at multiple situations; what works in one environment may or may not be effective in another environment. For instance, you may receive an email with an emoticon of a face with a frown. You can likely hear from a person's tone he is frowning when you are on the phone. When you're face to face, you have the added advantage of seeing flushing, frowning, fisting, and fighting stances. This helps you gauge if he is getting upset. You may also note a flickering smile that indicates he is not as serious as the words he is using during the negotiation.

SUBDUING A BULLY

There are a couple of models that apply to subduing a bully: the contending model and the pincer moves. A contending model is one that seeks to persuade the other party to agree to a solution you favor. This is also called "positional bargaining." Some of the tactics used in this model include inflated demands, irrevocable commitments, persuasion, and threats.[3]

Law enforcement personnel may encounter contention in a hostage situation. Hostage-takers want to be in control, and may demand a million dollars, a fully fueled jet, and the promise of immunity from prosecution. The negotiations center around these inflated demands until the negotiators can gain control and secure the safety of the hostages.

The pincer move evolved from military strategy. The goal is to encircle the enemy forces to cut off their path of retreat. Applied to negotiating with a hostage-taker, the law enforcement personnel may attempt to force a hostage-taker out in the open by shutting off electricity, food, and water. This is intended to apply pressure, to make the situation more urgent, and help the hostage-taker realize he is losing control of the situation. Such tactics are employed to drive the point home that the hostage-taker is being confronted by a force he will not be able to overcome.

A bully uses tactics like those of a hostage-taker. Hence, some of the tactics used in hostage situations can be employed against bullies.

SHOW OF FORCE

Sometimes a bully will use a show of force if negotiating does not work. In a well-publicized 2017 event, United Airlines wanted to fly four crew members on an already-full flight. After asking for and not getting volunteers to give up their seats, they picked four people at random. Three of them left the plane but the fourth was a physician who refused because he needed to see patients the following day.

Three Chicago airport police officers were involved in a show of force: large men standing in a narrow aisle to remove the passenger. The doctor's refusal in the face of this overwhelming force showed the intimidation did not work. A passenger captured video of the policemen dragging Dr. David Dao off the plane after he declined to give up his seat. Dr. Dao lost teeth and suffered a broken nose and a concussion. The incident generated much negative publicity for the airline, a drop in stock value, changes in overbooking procedures, and a rapid settlement with Dr. Dao for an undisclosed amount.[4]

In a negotiation with a bully you might say, "Wait, let's see how we can work this out so everybody is satisfied." Be careful of how you position yourself when confronted by what appears to be an overwhelming force. See if you can talk your way out of a situation. For example, a seven-year-old boy who was confronted by a bully called on his friends to be his bodyguards. The bully left him alone after that.

MIND YOUR BODY LANGUAGE

Up until now I have primarily focused on the bully's body language. Let's flip it and say you are the negotiator on the other side of the table with the bully. What body language should you display as you are interacting with a bully? You're negotiating with a hard-nose bully negotiator who believes that he wins when others lose. Let's look at that perspective first. In that environment if he leans forward, you should lean forward. Suppose he gives you a threatening ultimatum: "This is a take-it-or-leave-it offer" and he leans forward as he's saying so. You can lean forward and say something like, "I guess I'll just have to leave it." Notice the word choice.

If he pounds the table as he's talking, you can pound the table right back. If he says, "I could give a damn about this," you can say right back to him, "That makes two of us." Notice that what you're doing is mirroring his body language gestures. You're using words that imply, almost as strongly as he is, that you are digging in your heels too. Be careful when doing that; it may lead to a stalled negotiation.

Consider a situation in which someone is a "I'll go along to get along" type of negotiator. In that case, the person leans forward and says, "You know, I'm somewhat afraid this is the best offer and if you can't accept this we might not be able to come to a successful negotiation outcome."

His tone and demeanor are soft. You decide to lean away from him to convey your lack of interest in proceeding with the negotiation. Your reaction depends on where you are in the negotiation and how you want to influence that person. As you stay reclined, you could say, "I don't know. Do you see any other possibilities we might be able to engage in to make this a *more* (start to move forward as you say "more") successful negotiation outcome?" The timing of the movement from being reclined to moving forward as you are saying "more successful outcome" conveys the sentiment nonverbally that you are moving more literally and physically to what you are trying to achieve as a successful negotiation outcome.

The other negotiator may subconsciously react to your nonverbal gesture of moving forward as you pronounce the word "more." It will have some bearing on his mindset simply because even if it's subconscious it will register with that negotiator. Use the same tonality and pace as he is using so you give him the impression of mirroring him without him being aware that you're doing so.

The affinity principle is, "People like people who are like themselves." That is true whether you negotiate with a hard-nosed negotiator or a "I'll go along to get along" type of negotiator. The body language cues and clues you send convey your sentiments and perception of what's being offered or taken off the table. The hard-nosed negotiator makes the statement, "I just don't think we're going to come to a satisfactory conclusion today if you can't accept this offer." Instead of saying anything you just start packing up your things.

Take note of how far he may let you walk toward the door before saying anything or *if* he says anything at all. If he doesn't say anything, he has assured you through his nonverbal action he is ready to let you walk out. At least you know where you stand.

On the other hand, remember you haven't responded at all. No action is an action; that's something you always must consider. If you haven't responded and that action says, "I heard what you said," you're at least acknowledging you heard what he said. As you're walking toward the door you are saying, "If that is your best offer and you say that we can't come to an amicable solution to this negotiation, I'm willing to accept your position and I'm literally walking away."

Your body language provides nonverbal messages and reinforces your verbal messages. This adds more strength to your statements than if you had chosen to say, "I guess we're not going to conclude this negotiation." What you're communicating is there's nothing else to talk about so you're not going to continue to deliberate.

VERIFYING THE BULLY'S MINDSET

It is essential to understand the mindset of the bully and make sure your perceptions are accurate so you can predict what he might do based on your actions or to get him to perform certain actions. If you can make a prediction of what he will do if you stimulate him in a specific manner, you have better control of the negotiation. As an example, suppose you project your body language to depict yourself as a non-confrontational person. He recognizes that and thinks he can use that as a weapon in the negotiation by confronting you.

You may allow him to do that because you know that's the mindset he has about you. You could have intentionally primed his mindset to make him perceive you as a non-threatening, non-confrontational negotiator. As you can see how he's going to use that tool against you, you can understand his negotiation strategy. As the negotiation proceeds, you decide you no longer wish to appear non-confrontational. Let's say you start getting louder by just a few decibels. The bully thinks, "Wait a minute. I have miscalculated how I'm going to engage with this person. What else have I misjudged about my strategies and how I think he will react based on what I say?"

The better you understand the mindset of the other negotiator, especially if you sense that he's going to try to bully you, the better you can create the type of verbal and non-verbal responses needed to combat him.

I was talking to the manager of the sales department of a car dealer (I'll call it Dealer A) where I intended to buy a car. I observed his body language as he told me about all the perks of driving such a car, how people would see me, and the car's options. He smiled and looked off into the distance as he tilted his head. He used one hand to sweep across the imaginary spectrum of time. I perceived the gesture as implying that's the way people would view me as they saw me driving the car. I also knew he was attempting to put me in the frame of mind of feeling good in that picture. He never bothered to ask me what was important to me, so that told me he didn't care about my desires about a car.

The manager showed me through those actions what his mindset was. No matter how good of a deal he said this was (and he kept dropping the price), I still held back. I just sat there almost in a trance. I carefully kept a neutral expression on my face. "Yeah, okay, whatever," was the body language gesture I was conveying by sitting with my hands close to my body. I had my feet crossed at the time, although he couldn't see that. I let him go on and on. Finally, he said, "That's the best offer." He started listing every concession he had made (having never once asked me what I wanted in a car). His determination was to sell this car and I saw that in him, so I made him convince me why I should buy that car at his lowest price.

Here's where confirmation comes in when negotiating. The manager told me that he had offered me his best deal and the final number was substantially down from the one that he had initially quoted, which I appreciated.

When you're negotiating you need to know to what degree a good deal is a good deal. Before I agreed to his price I wanted to confirm it was indeed a good one. The only way to do that was to validate it was indeed a good deal through another source. I had already created a relationship with a salesperson at another dealership (Dealer B) and I really appreciated the candor of Dealer B's employee.

I had reason to trust him. He had built up his credibility over time. One time when I took my automobile to Dealer B the people in the service department told me if I tried to drive the car another mile it would blow up on me. I'm exaggerating slightly, but it was a dire situation that they described. I told the salesperson what his service department had told me. He started chuckling and said, "Greg, I apologize for that. These guys are just trying to get the car in there." He said, "Man, you can go drive that car for probably 100,000 miles and nothing will happen" and I said, "Thank you." He had already built credibility in my mind with his candor.

Recall I went to Dealer A to have this interaction with the manager of the sales department. I called the salesperson at Dealer B to tell him about the deal. He went on the computer and looked up the pricing of the car. When he called me back he said, "Greg, that is an awesome deal. If I were you, I would take it. We can't come anywhere close to that deal." I thanked him for his honesty. I bought the car from Dealer A. But I went back to my contact at Dealer B anyway. I shook his hand and gave him a $100 bill as a token of my appreciation; that was my way of keeping a loyal and trusted resource loyal to me. (When you find such resources, find a way to keep them loyal to you.)

A bully will display his mindset by his actions. That is something you should always be aware of. Don't listen to words. Watch actions. Actions will disclose a mindset much more so than words will.

THE BULLY'S PERCEPTION OF TARGETS

Who gets targeted? Depending on the bully's personality type, the bully will pick on someone who he or she knows will be less likely to respond, or to cause the bully to incur embarrassment. The bully prefers victims who are not confrontational. This fuels a perception the bully can push the victim indefinitely.

Contrast that with someone who the bully pushes to the point of re-sistance. The bully may stop and realize, "Whoa. Wait a minute. I think I may be coming close to a line I don't want to cross. I'll leave this person alone." The bully's perceptions are driven by the target's responses based on what the bully will do to that person.

THE TARGET'S PERCEPTION OF THE BULLY

The bully usually has an awareness of how the target sees the bully. In some cases, the bully may be seeking nothing more than respect, admiration, and acknowledgement of his presence. If the target does not give that to the bully, the bully may repeat his actions to get the target to respect him.

As kids, we called this "dissing you." What that meant was we didn't show the person the proper level of respect. In some cases, this was all it took for someone to become confrontational: "You didn't say 'excuse me' when you brushed by me." "Oh, I'm sorry," you respond. "It's too late now," he says as he punches you in the mouth.

SPEECH CLUES

The pace and tone of speech are a specific type of body language. The pace of speech is a clue in a verbal format that gives insight into the thought process of the other negotiator. If a person starts speaking a lot faster than he previously did, note what was said prior to that. What may have caused the individual to start speaking faster?

Slower speech may mean the other negotiator is in thought mode. This implies the person may be analyzing what you're saying more so than what he or she had been doing previously and could indicate a de-escalation of the bully's behavior.

Listen to the tone of the voice of the other negotiator. A drop in a person's voice at the end of a sentence communicates more of an emphatic point that the person is trying to make. If it goes up it tends to sound like a question.

In a situation in which a woman feels another person is being overly aggressive, she should take note of the bully's pace and tone. Notice I didn't say "bullying" in this case but rather "overly aggressive." The perception of bullying is in the eyes of the person who is being bullied as well as the person who is sending those signals. It is important how she says, "You better stop that right now." A deeper stern voice conveys the message better than a laugh and a chuckle. The former will have more of an impression on the mind of the person who's being aggressive than the latter. The little chuckle and the light-heartedness in the tone negates the message and conveys, "Maybe I don't want you to stop being overly aggressive."

If you want to send a strong message (especially as a woman dealing with overly aggressive or bullying behavior), use your tone of voice to forcefully say, "Stop it now!" Notice how you use just a few words. "Stop it now!" is definitive, as opposed to "If you don't stop this now it may lead to a position where we can be in trouble or I might think you're attempting to bully me." Your message must be strong if you really want the action you're seeking to stop when you're being bullied or being addressed in an overly aggressive manner.

RESPECT OR DISRESPECT THROUGH BODY LANGUAGE

Let's say you're in a face-to-face environment and the bully is saying, "We have about an hour to conclude this deal." His tone and pace convey a sense of wanting to pressure you. He is abrupt and demanding.

You decide to show disrespect by ignoring his statement. You are reading something unrelated to the negotiation. You toss the reading material aside and sit back in the chair with your hands clasped behind your neck, which is a sign of "I'm in control mode, I'm in thought mode, and I'm in everything is beautiful mode." You could reply by saying something like "Yeah, okay."

Now the bully is thinking to himself, "Wait a minute. What do you mean 'Yeah, okay'? I just made a statement about time. You're just going to reply by saying 'Yeah, okay' and you're not lending attention to what I'm saying. You look like you have all the time in the world." All those signals are saying that you are not really invested in this negotiation, nor are you attentive to what the bully just said. Your response could rile up a bully. If that was your intent, you were successful.

Think about how you can use your body language to silently combat a bully. The bully says, "We have to wrap this negotiation up because we're getting close to our time deadline." You can sit forward as you respond, "I agree with you" and see what the bully says next. You're again letting the bully control the pace of the negotiation. You can be doing so to see exactly how far he will take the negotiation or what he will do next with you agreeing with him.

The body language of sitting forward says, "I'm paying attention to what you're saying. What's next? Come on." You can add more emphasis to your body language of sitting up at that time by quickly saying, "I agree with you." You're to-the-point and using the quickness of the words as a sign that you realize the time factor here. You're agreeing with the person to see his next move.

The bully says, "I need you to sign on the dotted line right now to conclude this deal and both of us will walk away happy." One tactic I've used in a case such as this, when the other negotiator proposes both of us will walk away happy with the deal, is to respond, "Let me ask you: Is this a deal you would accept if it was reversed?" That is a trap that is very difficult to elude because if the bully says, "Yes, I would accept it," the bully has just given you the right to flip the deal.

Let's say the deal was tilted 60/40 with 60 percent in the bully's favor and 40 percent in your favor. The bully has now said, "Yes, I would accept the deal if it was 60 percent in your favor and 40 percent in mine." Your next question is, "How about if we do that and I can sign on the dotted line?" Of course, the bully realizes he's now in a no-win situation. You've put him in a box and he is going to seek a way to kick himself out of the box. It behooves you to observe how he does so. "You know I can't accept that," he replies.

"Then why would you expect me to accept it?" you ask in a more forceful manner and using a tone that conveys you are throwing up your hands as you ask the question. Your reaction is something the bully must grapple with to make progress in the negotiation.

PICKING YOUR WORDS

Pick your words carefully when you're addressing a bully. Suppose the bully says, "I'll kick your butt." He may be referring to physical violence or using the term to refer to besting you in a negotiation. Imagine he says it in a very strong manner. You can challenge him by saying something such as, "And what do you think I'll be doing while you're kicking my butt?"

You mirrored his use of the word "butt" just like he used it. Your message leaves him thinking, "This guy is not just going to sit there and allow me to kick his butt without some type of fight or without some form of resistance. Maybe I better reassess how I'm going to manage this situation."

How you respond and the body language you display will depend on where you are in the negotiation and what you want to occur next. Your strategy will show if you're willing to be more confrontational, less confrontational, or willing to acquiesce altogether based on your objectives for the negotiation.

The bully might say, "This has been a tough negotiation. I think we are near a successful outcome." You can smile at the bully and reply, "I agree with you. This has been a tough negotiation. You are a tough negotiator, my friend. I appreciate someone who really knows how to dig his heels in while attempting to lead the other person in the negotiation."

Observe how this response praised the other negotiator; a lot of bullies thrive off of praise. You also acknowledged the fact that what he said was valid. You could have used the exact opposite words and used a lot of weak words and phrases: "You know I think you're a nasty piece of work, to be frank with you, but I'll tell you sometimes it takes a nasty person to negotiate in a hard manner to get a successful negotiation outcome." Here are some examples of phrases you should avoid.

- ▶ "I think we can do this."
- ▶ "Maybe this might be the outcome we could reach if we do this."
- ▶ "I'm not sure if this is the right direction to go in."
- ▶ "I *don't believe* I can do that."

All those words make you appear weaker as opposed to:

- ▶ "We can do this."
- ▶ "That's what I would accept."
- ▶ "This is the direction that we should go in."
- ▶ "This will be a positive outcome."

When you speak with definitive words you lend more strength to your statement as opposed to "maybe," "possibly," or "it could occur." If your strategy is to not appear weak use precise, strong words.

PICKING YOUR DEMEANOR

Let's think about the demeanor you should display when you're dealing with a bully. When you're talking about any type of demeanor you're going to display, it should be one that adds value to your overall negotiation plan. If you're talking about adopting a combative demeanor to deal with a bully, you should be prepared to display such an aggressive demeanor in levels. You might even label them on a scale from 1 to 10.

A "Level 1" could be mildly increasing the volume of your voice to show you disagree. A "Level 10" could be outright screaming at her.

You might also consider displaying a demeanor that's acquiescent to the bully to see what she might possibly do. In that case your demeanor might be somewhat bashful as you speak. You deliberately display body language that involves drawing yourself inward. Your hands are closer to you; your legs are closed. Your feet are closer to you as you are speaking in subdued tones and constraining your gestures. The bully interprets your actions as holding your cards close to your chest. That could make the bully start to wonder what else is going on in your mind. This may distract her from her aggressive position.

Always consider mirroring what the bully is doing. By doing so you may feel what's going on in the bully's mind (referring to the kinesthetic perspective). If you are really attuned to that person, you can understand his thought processes and what he is getting ready to do. In that way, you validate how your actions are influencing the bully.

- ► What does he do next?
- ► Does he become milder?
- ► Does he become angrier?

Next, reassess how your actions caused his reactions. Did you achieve what you expected to get? Did the bully react in a predictable way? Do you think his reactions were contrived or genuine?

There's always the opportunity for a bully to misinterpret your body language. When you sense that's happening, how do you alter it to make it more effective? Maybe the first question is: How do you know a bully is misinterpreting your body language? You've likely seen the cartoon character of the dog with the inquisitive look on his face, his head cocked to one side. People display the same type of look when they are confused. The body language gesture consists of slight closing of the eyes, a tilting of the head, and the lips open. The upper lip tends to be up a little bit while the bottom lip is down, which means the mouth is slightly gaped, adding to an inquisitive look.

If you see that curious look, you know the person is wondering, "What am I sensing? What's happening at this particular point in time?"

Also, if you sense that you can pose the questions "What are you thinking?" and "What does that mean?" You will get more insight about how the bully is responding to your actions in the negotiation.

If you sense he misinterprets your actions, encourage him to ask for clarification: "Are you unclear about what I am saying? What are you sensing? How can I clarify this for you?" You can then address his direct concerns based on the words he's using.

Here's a negotiation tactic you would use if he posed such questions to you. The question to him would be: "What are you sensing?" Let him give you more input about what he's thinking. The more input you get from him the better you can know to what degree he is misinterpreting your body signals.

Confirm what he has said to you and what he's perceiving by doing the exact same thing: projecting the same image you projected a moment ago and see how he responds. That will serve as a point of reference to how you can use the same body language gesture to convey the strategy you've now tied to that gesture. Emotionally and subliminally you have now formed a relationship between your body language and the strategy.

Those are some of the ways you can understand and reshape his perspective based on his interpretation of your body language gestures.

BULLIES IN THEIR ENVIRONMENT

Let's focus on the environment the bully is in. The environment could be anywhere from a dark street corner to a brightly lit boardroom. There is a difference in the way you use your body language based on the environment you are in.

For instance, Harvey Weinstein's environment consisted of private hotel rooms where he employed the "the casting couch." He and others have been accused of using their power positions to request or demand sexual favors in exchange for attention or privileges. Harvey promised roles in Hollywood movies in exchange for sexual activities. This tactic made women feel pressured to decide if they wanted to go along to get along.

The bully feels safest and more secure in his own environment. Harvey felt more powerful when he was in a hotel room with an actress or would-be actress. Be more mindful of negotiating with people in their environment. You've heard the term "home-team advantage." When a negotiator is in his "home environment" he can use that to affect the outcome of the negotiation.

The sexual predator would likely select an environment where detection or interruption of the act is unlikely. The target's vulnerability skyrockets when the predator manipulates a situation to be alone with the target. Acknowledging the risks to the young models, *Conde Nast* issued a set of guidelines to protect them by stating, "All models appearing in fashion shoots must be eighteen years of age or older. The only exceptions will be those appearing as themselves as part of a profile or new story, and they will be required to have a chaperone on set at all times."[4]

Former U.S.A. Gymnastics physician Larry Nassar has been accused of sexually assaulting 140 women, according to the statement of one of the athletes. He called it "medical treatment." One of the athletes, Mckayla Maroney, reported that during the 2011 Olympics, Dr. Nassar gave her a sleeping pill. The fifteen-year-old awoke in his hotel bed to find him giving her "a treatment." She said, "People should know that this is not just happening in Hollywood. This is happening everywhere. Wherever there is a position of power, there seems to be potential for abuse. I had a dream to go to the Olympics, and the things that I had to endure to get there were unnecessary and disgusting." Nassar pleaded guilty to federal child pornography charges, and was sentenced to sixty years in prison.[6]

When you are negotiating with a bully in his environment, use your body language to assert your power to counter the bully's power. You can project body language gestures, such as crossing your arms when you're in his environment and frowning. Think about a cluster of signals to use in the bully's environment. You can take away the power of the bully even when you're in his environment by sending out body language signals like a frown, crossing the arms, and standing directly on both feet with your weight equally distributed. You can strengthen your posture by having your fist balled and your arms are crossed. Doing so would add more emphasis to your actions. That indicates, "I'm ready to take some form of action. Now back off, don't mess with me."

Be mindful of the environment you negotiate in so you can be stronger based on how you position yourself. Don't smile as much if you're in a threatening environment. Stay out of certain environments, such as those with the bully's allies. The presence of the bully's allies weakens you. (Do you get a mental picture of a bully surrounded by bodyguards?)

Confront the bully when he feels weakest. This requires knowing his mindset, including whether he is performing for people who influence his actions in his environment. Are there people whose recognition and praise he wants? For example, he might crave his employer's praise. "You did a fantastic job of beating down that vendor's price." Listen to the bully's words and watch his body language. Is he using less powerful expressions? He might say, "Well, maybe if you did this we could agree" as opposed to "This is what you should do!"

Look for body language signals when he's speaking to you. Suppose he's looking around to see who else might be listening or who might overhear the two of you if you're face to face. That implies he doesn't want others to hear what's being said because the listeners are witnesses. For example, the bully plans to deny ever agreeing to your terms and does not want another person to be able to corroborate the terms of the agreement. If you sense that, you can imply you are recording the conversation by tapping your briefcase or purse.

You may recall President Trump calling the then-FBI Director James Comey into a private one-on-one meeting in which the president was alleged to have asked Comey to back off from an investigation that was targeting former National Security Adviser Michael Flynn. When Comey testified about the occurrence, President Trump said Comey was fabricating the situation. Trump tweeted, "James Comey better hope that there are no 'tapes' of our conversations before he starts leaking to the press!"[7] To that, Comey replied, "Lordy, I hope there are recordings."[8]

The point is, in today's technological environment, you could easily have your phone recording a conversation. Know the type of bully you are dealing with and be prepared to address his future actions by positioning yourself properly today. When you are in the bully's environment, keep these guidelines in mind:

▶ Don't position yourself as being confrontational; doing so can escalate a situation. You want to be the one controlling an escalation.

▶ If a bully attempts to use bullying tactics against you and others are around, note the bully's body language to determine the show he's putting on for their behalf. Specifically watch to see if he looks around at those in attendance when he attempts these tactics; he'll be looking for their approval to assess if he should continue.

▶ Take note of the nonverbal responses they make and what they say, such as "Oh" or "Go get him." Nonresponsive audiences take some of the energy away from the bully.

These body language gestures give you insight into what the bully is thinking.

There are ways to use the body language of others to combat a bully even when they're not around. To do this, you need to be familiar with the people the bully respects or sees as allies. Mimic their body language to convey your association with those who the bully *respects*.

If you adopt the same body language of those who the bully has *bullied* in the past, the bully gets the signal that you are like his prior victims.

Adopting body language positions of strength is effective because it reminds the bully of body language he's seen in the past that he respects and recognizes as being a strong position.

In Conclusion

A bully does not want to pick on a strong target; that's too much work for him in a negotiation and in life. Carefully watch the bully's body language so you have insight as to where the discussion is headed and how to de-escalate a situation.

Always make sure you have back up in the form of anything that bully would see as something he might have to contend with. Use your body language so a bully will not see you as the target. If he does, and tries to bully you, be prepared. Position yourself so you don't appear weak. When you can shape your persona as one not to be messed with, you will always come out a lot further ahead. Now add to that persona the fact you are fair. You treat others with respect. A bully will hesitate before attacking you. He may realize he would be laughed at for trying to best you.

I have additional resources about interpreting body language on my website: *http://themasternegotiator.com/negotiating-with-a-bully*.

HOMEWORK

Over the next twenty-one days, make a special effort to observe the body language of random people, and those who you know, in fifteen-minute segments throughout the day; do this three to five times throughout the day.

The purpose of this exercise is to make you more aware of the body language signals people emit. In the case of observing people you know, you can validate your perceptions by asking if what you perceived was accurate.

I engage in this exercise from time to time to continuously strengthen my own abilities of reading body language. Sometimes I do so by walking up to strangers in airports, concerts, and other gatherings where crowds of people assemble. I introduce myself, tell them what I observed, and ask if they'd give me their brief feedback. Some of the feedback has led to some very interesting conversations.

As you increase your ability to decipher body language signals, you will become more astute about the hidden thoughts motivating the actions of the subjects you observe. That will in turn increase your overall abilities at the negotiation table.

3

Strategies: Fighting Back

Recognizing the signs of a bully's demeanor helps you prepare to confront him. Way before you get to the negotiation table, you should observe their mannerisms, style of interaction, and so on. Interaction styles are some of the things you should observe about someone who has a bullying demeanor. By observing those nuances, you will have a more effective way to prepare for how you're going to confront him.

If, for example, the individual happens to be someone who you know, no matter how much proof you show, he will not back away from the story he already presented. You will need a different negotiation approach with this individual. Prepare by observing how he acts in a normal environment over time; this will give you insight as to how to confront him.

Watch the bully to make sure you understand his demeanor and his patterns of behavior in certain situations. Then you can put a plan together as to how you're going to negotiate with this individual.

PICKING THE RIGHT DEMEANOR

The *right* demeanor is dependent upon the person with whom you're negotiating. In a lot of situations, a softcore bully will be someone who tests you to see how far she can push you. She's not that much of a bully. She's using bullying behavior as a tactic or a strategy. If you matched her demeanor she would more than likely back down as opposed to raising the stakes.

Now let's contrast that to someone who is a hardcore bully. This bully is someone who really doesn't care about you. She's going to display her dominance over you. Depending on the strategy you have laid out for the negotiation, you may decide to display a demeanor that is just as aggressive as the bully's. Or you might display one that's a little softer to see exactly how far she will push you based on how she has planned the negotiation. A handshake is a great example of this.

When President Trump met with President Emmanuel Macron of France and they shook hands, President Trump was extremely aggressive with his handshake and would not let President Macron's hand go. The handshake lasted twenty-nine seconds![1]

The person who is most dominant will be the one who will hold the handshake the longest. In return, President Macron shook President Trump's hand just as aggressively. The message being exchanged was something along the lines of "I am going to do exactly what I need to do to show you that I can be just as aggressive as you. I'm not going to back down from you. Do not try to intimidate me." President Macron adopted this demeanor simply to convey to President Trump that he would not be bullied and Trump shouldn't even try it.

The demeanor you adopt is one that needs to be designed to achieve the outcome you're seeking and to position you so the other person knows what may happen when attempting to bully you.

INTERACTING VERSUS NEGOTIATING WITH A BULLY

You may engage with a bully and think you're not be negotiating. Don't adopt that mindset. Remember, you're always negotiating; what you do today helps to create the environment for tomorrow's interactions. However, there is very little difference. A bully's behavior can indicate how he might act in a certain situation when you are not officially negotiating. This helps you to anticipate how you might respond to bullying tactics and to prepare a plan to implement a specific strategy.

Perhaps the bully is looking at you as a potential target. If he senses weakness, even though you're not officially negotiating with him, he can assemble strategies as to how he's going to manipulate you with his bullying.

Consider this situation: You are with a group of people who are waiting in line to get into a theater. A bully skips the line and walks to the front. If somebody objected to the bully going to the front of the line, that is a form of negotiation. In this situation you would have to be even more mindful of how you would interact with the bully. There are other people in the line who you don't know. Just the fact that those other people are present will influence the bully's behavior.

The bully may do things that are unexpected simply because he does not want to be embarrassed. After all, he thinks he's strong enough to jump in front of everybody and not have anybody challenge him. If you challenge him, be prepared to address him given the fact that others are there. Your interactions would likely be different in an environment where no one else is there.

Let's say you're the third person in front of the individual who the bully jumps in front of. If you don't say anything, the bully may note that and therefore you become a target for his bullying tactics.

BULLYING BEHAVIOR VERSUS MISUNDERSTANDING

In another situation, the person cutting in a line could do so for innocent reasons. A colleague of mine and her son were in California in line to board an aerial tramway. They didn't realize the line was coming in from the right as they walked straight up a set of steps to join the line. The back of the line was to their right. The sun was in their eyes. A woman very clearly said to the mother, "The back of the line is behind me. We are all waiting in the same line that you want to be in."

My colleague apologized and went to the back of the line. The woman who delivered the emphatic message was surrounded by other people who would have dissuaded a bully who deliberately cut into the line.

You can misinterpret somebody's reaction and identify them as a bully when they are not a bully. Be clear about the person's intent. The mother and son were not trying to jump the line and it was an honest mistake. Once they were informed where the line was, they apologized and went to the back.

If someone was trying to be a bully, he would say something like, "Mind your business. I don't care where the line is. What are you going to do?" That would be a direct challenge; you'd know for sure that person's position. You can tell by the person's reaction and actions to what degree he may be a bully.

I once had a similar experience. I had gotten almost to the front of the line when a woman looked at the line and decided she was going to cut in a few people in front of me. I politely said, "Excuse me, Miss, you may not be aware, but the end of the line is back there." She looked at me and her response was, "I'm not jumping in front of you. Don't say anything."

I thought to myself, "That's an odd statement. Does she not realize if I was fourth to be waited on next that now I'm fifth because she's there?" I also thought, "I'm not going to raise an issue here because she's a woman and I'm a man." I calculated it would not be in my best interest, especially because I was so close to the front of the line anyway. If we reverse the situation and she was a man, I might have said something stronger to him. I would have done so knowing I would have to control whatever results occurred because of my statement; that must be calculated when you're dealing with a bully or a suspected bully.

When I was young, the bigger kids would pick on the little kids because they knew the little kids did not have the power or strength that they had. The bigger kids would take the money of the little kids and beat them up. As some of the little kids got bigger (and in some cases got bigger than those who used to bully them), the bullies stopped messing with them. The bullies realized there was more of a challenge than they expected.

STRATEGIES FOR BULLY TYPES

Comprehending the motivations of bullies help you recognize their brain games. Consider the hardcore bully:

- ▶ How did he pick his target?
- ▶ Why did he select that person?
- ▶ Where is he using his bullying tactics?

This analysis gives insight into the bully so you can combat him. Saving face is important to the bully. He may become irrational if he feels as though he's backed into a corner. (Never back people physically or emotionally into a corner with no way out. They'll come out fighting. You don't want to trigger any actions you had not anticipated.)

Deciphering the mindset of the bully identifies the source of his motivation to bully you. In some cases, it may not be your personality that causes the bully to target you for his tactics. It may be due to your ethnicity, gender, sexual orientation, religion, or other attributes he does not like. Striking at you can be a way to strike at people he despises.

Knowing that about the bully gives you more insight as to how to combat his efforts. You can attempt to convey understanding if you sense he wishes to be understood, or attempt to give him information he can use to reassess his way of thinking. In either case, knowing why he has that mindset explains why he may attempt to bully you. You can shift his paradigm.

In a negotiation, understanding the opposing negotiator's mindset (that is, the way he thinks and why he thinks that way) is essential for the negotiation's progress. The insight about his thought process will allow you to determine if he places more value on his strength than on seeing if you will back down. If he places more of an emphasis on the former and not the latter, display strength, even in the face of what might be his tirades against you. His verbal aggression might be a test. He could be seeking to uncover your weakness. If he is successful at doing so, he would likely exploit your weak areas.

Bullies have fears. To understand what a bully fears gives a negotiator the ability to manipulate the situation to induce fear in the bully. A bully fears being bullied and/or appearing foolish when attempting to bully someone else.

CONFRONTING A BULLY DURING NEGOTIATION

How you confront a bully depends on several factors. One of them is whether there are others in the environment. Are they your allies or the bully's allies? If they are your allies, they present a force the bully must contend with as he interacts with you.

Let's switch the scenario and say he has allies who are present. Now he has support; he knows he can push a little bit harder because he has a little more strength behind his actions. His group may also egg him on to engage with you even more. The goal is clear that he wants to win. The bully may be the leader of the group or a follower.

In some street gangs there are initiation procedures that new gang members have to engage in just to prove that they are worthy of being in the gang. They are expected to do drastic things, such as committing a murder, because they need to show their future gang members that they are tough enough to be part of the group.

It's not just the bully whose behavior and reactions you need to consider. Everyone else in the previous line-cutting example was watching the interaction as the woman took charge and told my colleague that she was not in the right spot. Even though the woman just had her family around her, everyone else in line became part of the dynamics. They all wanted to leave as well. They would all support the person who spoke up.

Let's say the bully has three people with him who are physically bigger individuals. A person ready to confront the bully would assess the bully's powerful companions and question his or her own support. Consider the forces that may allow the bully to buttress his position when you're negotiating.

It is helpful when you can see the forces you're up against. However, they might be invisible. In today's environment some people have become emboldened to display a much stronger demeanor. For example, in certain parts of the United States people can carry concealed weapons. A guy who is 5'4" and weighs 150 pounds may take on someone who is much bigger because the smaller guy has a concealed weapon.

Be mindful of what you're not seeing when you're negotiating with a bully who suddenly becomes more aggressive. Observe the bully's normal behavior and then compare that to how she is acting. You will gain additional insight about whether there is a silent force you are not seeing that could be affecting the bully's behavior.

Be very mindful of not only how you display your intentions but also of the environment you're in when you're doing so. For example, suppose when I was a kid I accidently stepped on a bully's toe. Depending on the environment I was in that event might trigger a fight. Even if I said, "I'm sorry" I might have gotten punched.

Understand the environment in which you will engage with a bully before thinking about doing so and consider the unseen forces that may be influencing the bully's behavior. It would be best to do so before you even enter that environment. Out of self-preservation, avoid environments in which the bully would have additional support or make sure you have support when confronting a bully.

Be ready to back away from a negotiation if the person with whom you are negotiating is so hard-nosed that it's going to take too much effort to get the reward you're seeking from the negotiation.

You can test a bully's demeanor and how dominantly he wants to portray himself just by posing soft questions to him. For example, you might say, "Excuse me, sir," as opposed to "Yo! Hey guy!" Consider your intonation. You can say "sir" in a forceful way or a soft way. You're conveying your sentiments and positioning yourself by the way you speak.

ESCALATION OF A NEGOTIATION

It is not only awareness of the environment, but who's in the environment that affects the bully's behavior. Is there a probability of the situation escalating to a point where it may get out of control? Will you allow it to escalate before you just back off? If you do, what impact will that have on future interactions with the bully? How well can you predict the way it might flare up?

You might be confronted with a potentially violent situation and you must intervene. For instance, you recognize the bully is about ready to strike somebody. Security guards, police officers, and psychiatric nurses are usually trained in how to subdue a person. One of my colleagues was in a restaurant with her husband who had been trained to intervene in violent situations. A man came into the restaurant with a golf club. As he pulled it back to hit the waitress, my colleague's husband immediately confronted the man. He knew how to disarm him, bring him to the ground, and get him under control. Similarly, there is a frightening element of risk when you interact with a bully or in how you confront them.

A bully who misinterprets your actions or intent when you confront that person can turn the encounter into an out-of-control situation. Suppose the bully is being aggressive and you're standing five feet apart. The bully takes a step toward you and angrily says, "What did you say?" That's a different demeanor she is projecting versus standing in the same place and saying, "I'm sorry, excuse me. Can you please repeat that?" A bully who is taking a step closer to you is saying, "I'm one step closer to possibly becoming more aggressive."

In such a case you can turn around and say, "I'm sorry. What I was trying to say was. . . ." Again, be careful about how you speak. Your tone will convey an additional message on top of your words. Suppose you had emphatically or sarcastically commented something like "You heard what I said." You put your hands on your hips and used your body language to say, "What, you want to do something about it?" You are now being more definitive in sending a message: "Hey bully, if you don't like what I said I can be more aggressive." You're in control. A full outright confrontation hasn't occurred at that point, but at the same time you must be very aware of what your next action should be.

In the heat of the moment most people do not think. They react. They're watching the body language of the bully and the bully is watching the body language of the potential target. All your efforts should be coordinated to address misinterpretations of your message. Clarify them and state them more firmly to make your message clear. Keep these body language gestures and non-verbal gestures in mind as you are involved in a confrontation.

You can convey respect for a bully through nonverbal gestures, but be careful. Don't lean in too close. The bully may interpret your body language as threatening. Show that you are really paying attention to what he is saying. Also, be aware of your facial expressions and keep them congruent with your verbal messages.

For example, if he says something like, "If you don't take this offer I will walk away from the negotiation table. I will destroy you and your company, and that will be the end of your business life," you lean into him and say, "Do it!" You've shown that you were listening to him and challenging him with that response as opposed to saying, "Wow, that sounds very extreme. Why are you adopting that position?"

You've again conveyed the fact that you're listening to him. You're giving him respect in both situations, but you're also projecting a different demeanor by your actions. You're repositioning the bully: "I respect what you're saying, but at the same time I am limiting you as to how much I am going to allow you to bully me. I've just shown through my actions how I might acquiesce, or not, to your demands. I am calling your bluff."

You can take this position if you're standing face to face. You can just say, "Look I know this is serious." Put your hands together in front of your chest to form a steeple. That projects a position of authority while not proclaiming one. At the same time through that body language and the tonality in your voice you convey you are taking what he's saying seriously. You are also listening and offering him the level of respect his words are demanding. You may not want to do that because it doesn't suit your purposes. Of course, you may do so for the moment just to watch the bully's reaction to gain insight about what you think he will do next. You're still giving him respect while at the same time positioning yourself for whatever it is you wish to do next.

WATCHING THE BULLY'S BEHAVIORAL CLUES

Consider the clues you should be looking for to get a sense of how the bully perceives your actions. In a previous example, I described a situation in which the bully took a step toward you and said, "What did you say?" Should you take a step backward? That conveys, "I'm ready to retreat." The bully will perceive your message based on your body language.

Using the earlier example of the mother and son who inadvertently cut into the line, suppose the mother reacted differently. Instead of apologizing to the lady who informed her they were cutting in, the mother walked right up to her. Let's say she got within six inches of her face and said to her, "Thank you very much. I appreciate that." And then she stood there for a moment to see what the lady would do. Her words were conciliatory, but her body language was confrontational. Others in the vicinity might have jumped in at that point. If the lady slightly backed away she would be conveying she saw the mother as being much more hard-nosed. If the mother and son wanted to stay in line where they were, they would do so.

You can observe the body language of a bully, especially at the negotiation table, to sense exactly how he's going to respond based on how he perceives your actions. Leaning away from the negotiation table is a sign that says, "I don't want to be as close to this situation as I am." Rubbing the eye is a sign that communicates "I don't want to see what's about to happen." Rubbing the ear means "Did I really hear that right? I don't believe I'm actually hearing this." Understand also that one body language gesture alone does not validate what you sense. Observe gestures in clusters. For example, if someone rubbed his ear and backed away from the negotiation table at the same time, that would serve as further confirmation he did not believe what he was hearing or saying.

Observe body language to discern what the other negotiator is thinking. Once such gestures are observed, you can use that time to divert his attention to something that is more advantageous to your position.

Take care when dealing with a hardcore bully. If it serves you, give him the respect that he seeks. Also let him know that he can't bully you. Marshall real or imaginary forces to turn the dynamics to your favor.

Observe the bully's behavior to determine how you're getting through to that person. Is what you're saying having an impact? When you steeple your hands you are actually saying to him "I understand what you're saying." You are conveying through the hands gesture and the tone of your voice you are being respectful. You are intently listening. Adopting this body language may be very effective in helping the bully perceive you are paying attention and ready to defuse the situation. The bully may respond, "I can appreciate that you understand and are ready to negotiate." Always be aware of how your body language gestures are being interpreted. Some bullies may interpret the steeple gesture as a sign of praying versus authority. What the bully says and does next will give you insight about how he interprets your actions.

USING YOUR BEHAVIOR TO CUE THE BULLY

Speak softly and more slowly to calm a bully down. When the bully responds, you are having some influence on the bully. If you are standing nose to nose, use a soft tone to say something like, "Look, we don't have to escalate the situation." Ideally the bully takes a step back and agrees.

As a young boy, when neither of two people wanted to back down they would be face to face. To deescalate a situation, one kid might say something similar to, "I don't have time to be messing with you right now." He may take a step back. If by chance the bully took a step forward, that might indicate the bully felt bolder by the other person backing away. If, on the other hand, the bully stayed still or also took a step back, you would know the bully was backing off.

In some situations, a person who blinks sends a signal. It could be interpreted as a challenge or a mandate. The bully blinks to show he is giving in to the other person's position. These are the types of signals you're looking for to see if you have an influence over the bully. They are some of the signs you can pick to gain insight into how the bully is truly responding.

STRATEGIES FOR COMBATTING BULLYING

So far, I have described the use of body language and the actions you can take to either placate or stand your ground when a person is becoming riled up by an interpretation of something that has happened. Assessing the intensity of the bully's reactions is essential.

In this model, you would use a scale of 1 to 10, with 10 being a bully who is just out to win at all costs. A person who is a "1" is just putting his proverbial toe in the water to test the situation.

With that scale in mind, suppose you know someone is at a Level 5 before a negotiation. You anticipate the bully will behave during the negotiation consistent with a Level 5, and may plan to escalate the situation, so you will enter the negotiation with a strategy of having more people on your side. Your support people will have more insight, and be perceived as being intellectually stronger, wealthier, or more powerful to help you achieve your desired outcome. In so doing, you can back the bully down or at least give the bully insight about the force he would have to confront to win. If you had more resources or forces with you than he had, you would be more strongly positioning yourself.

Let's flip that. Let's say you have the same situation where he's at a Level 5 and you want to see exactly what you can do before calling in reinforcements. You walk into the room with one associate and project a demeanor that says, "I'm an easy type of person to get along with." You see he goes from a Level 5 to a 6. The more you try to placate him the more he escalates. He goes to a Level 7. Unexpectedly, you intensify your strength. You either call in reinforcements or you change your demeanor to one in which you become the person who might be perceived as a bully behaving at a Level 8.

You can weave these strategies into a negotiation at different intervals if that suits you, but to do so means you need to know exactly what other forces he may be holding in reserve. Like a chess game, to enact any successful strategy you have to be thinking four, five, six, seven, and eight steps ahead. Anticipate how you would address certain situations.

That forms the strategy you assemble before even entering the negotiation with the bully.

Sometimes a bully in a key leadership position uses ploys to try to make himself look bigger. Why? He wants worldwide attention to show that he has validity; he has meaning in the world. He is playing an extremely dangerous game. He must show the generals in his army that he's a tough guy, lest they attack him from within. By identifying the possible reasons why a bully is displaying a demeanor you can be better prepared to create the appropriate strategy to deal with him.

Here's why a bully always must calculate to what degree an irrational opponent might suddenly do something that he has not anticipated, which is why bullying can be so damning for the bully. A war could result. That's why the bully must calculate exactly to what degree he will walk up to a line and not get close enough to be forced to or accidentally step over it.

This horrifying scenario constitutes the reality of nuclear power. And it is why we must be very mindful of how we negotiate with a bully. We can literally lose control of the negotiation simply because of unexpected things occurring. That's another reason why you should think multiple steps ahead about the strategy you're using to think through if this happens, here's what I'm going to do.

After the U.S. failed to overthrow the Castro regime in Cuba during the Bay of Pigs Invasion, the Soviet premier Nikita Khrushchev reached a secret agreement with Castro to place Soviet nuclear missiles in Cuba. Cuba began clearing land to construct several missile sites. When U.S intelligence discovered evidence of a missile build up, President Kennedy issued a public warning against the introduction of offensive weapons into Cuba. Despite the warning, five weeks later a U.S aircraft took pictures showing continued construction for missile launching sites. President Kennedy ordered a quarantine of Cuba and demanded that the Soviets dismantle the missile bases and return the weapons to the U.S.S.R. Through a series of direct and indirect communications, Kennedy and Khrushchev reached an agreement about the terms of resolving the crisis.[2]

MISDIRECTION TO DISTRACT OR CONFRONT A BULLY

Misdirection distracts a bully. The longer you can keep a bully occupied on something else, the less time he will have to focus on you. You can use others to attack the bully, use misinformation placed in strategic locations, or create angst within the bully's camp by causing mistrust amongst his allies.

Use body language to feign being aggressive to see exactly how the bully might react. You can also do so to imply "I don't like what you just said" or "I don't like the body language you just exhibited."

Any time you sense the bully is in a state of confusion and you know you will not be attacked, get out of the environment. Don't run, but walk away during the bully's moment of confusion or indecision. Use this opportunity to escape an environment that might otherwise cause you harm.

The same concept of escape applies during a negotiation, even if you must call it off at that moment you have positional power to do whatever serves you best. Recognize when those times occur. You will understand how to utilize them because you planned ahead.

Consider a situation in which you and the bully could potentially escalate into a confrontational stage. The bully puts his hands on his hips, which indicates a sense of readiness as he starts to frown and lean into you. You mimic those exact same gestures to the bully. What you're saying by sending such a signal in that case is, "I'm not going to back down, so if you're going to do something, bring it."

Now, if that was the bully's intent and you were just basically calling him out on it, that could be a ploy in the form of misdirection you were using just to get him to alter his position. That's why misdirection is so valuable in any negotiation and particularly when you're confronting a bully. It can also be dangerous if the bully takes you up on the threat.

If the bully sensed you are attempting to use misdirection, he may escalate the situation by doing something you had not accounted for.

That could cause things to escalate to a point that becomes uncomfortable and you lose control of the negotiation.

Be mindful as you attempt to employ a misdirection tactic in a negotiation as to what actions you expect the bully to take. Therefore, if you have multiple plans in place to combat the bully's different responses you can regain control of the negotiation faster.

As a negotiating strategy, misdirection is a strategy to get away from the current topic that's being discussed. You may use it simply because you need a breather. Let's say the negotiators have become exasperated to the point of anger. You can say something like, "I can sense that this is getting very heated. Can we please just take a break for a moment? It's such a lovely day and a lovely day just puts me in a better frame of mind. Can we go outside and walk in the sun for a moment?" A change in environment will change the dynamics of a negotiation. Be mindful of using an environmental change to enhance the strategy of using misdirection in your negotiations.

The misdirection in that case is to alleviate pressure from the current situation. Walking out in the sunshine may invoke a more pleasant mindset. That's a time of happiness versus if it was a rainy day. Misdirection can be used to *de-escalate* a situation.

Now let's talk about misdirection to *escalate* a situation. Suppose you have an opponent who is trying to bully you and has said in a negotiation, "I'll close your business down." This happened to one of my colleagues. Larry was a lawyer who was negotiating on behalf of his client to purchase a building. Larry did not know that Maria, the building owner, had nothing to lose because she really did not have a stake in the business housed in the building.

The lawyer was trying to use bullying tactics about the dollar amount to be offered for the building. He used a misdirection of trying to paint how gloomy the situation could be if his client decided not to buy the building. He kept using wording such as "You might end up not getting as much money for the property. Boy, it's going to be much tougher to sell if that's the case. You're going to have to hold on to it longer."

In this situation the lawyer was using misdirection to paint a gloomier environment of what could occur if the building was not sold. Larry started making demands that were just completely out of the realm of possibility. Maria hung up the phone on the him.

Here's what you should be concerned about when using misdirection:

- ▶ How far should you take it?
- ▶ To what degree will you use it?
- ▶ What is its purpose?
- ▶ How will you recover if misdirection gets out of hand?

Misdirection is a way to alter course of the negotiation. Parents of small children use misdirection all the time to try to distract them from something the child finds more appealing than what the parent is asking the child to do. By posing something as an attractive alternative the parent can distract that child away from the activity that is undesirable. "Let's work on this puzzle" (to get him away from the hot stove).

Misdirection is a tactic that can be effective in everyday life. Consider this fictional situation: Joseph and Carly sat at their booth in the restaurant. As Joseph glanced at his cell phone to check the time, Carly inwardly groaned. She watched her husband's eyes tighten and he started to breathe heavily. Carly had gotten used to recognizing the signs of her husband's temper. "Here we go again," she thought. "Carly, do you realize it has been thirty-four minutes since we ordered and we have not even gotten the first course? I really want to say something to our waiter."

"Why can't we have a simple, relaxing dinner?" she wondered. Knowing the best way to handle the situation was to distract him, Carly changed the subject to their upcoming vacation. The time flew by as she engaged him in an animated discussion of what they could do while away. When the food arrived ten minutes later, Joseph barely glanced at it before continuing his thought.

That's a misdirection, but nobody called it as such. What we should be mindful of since you're always negotiating is that what you do today influences tomorrow's actions and outcomes.

Car dealers do it too. When you go to buy a car, they show you this fantastic-looking car and it's the one that you know that you just must have. The sticker price is a whole lot more expensive than what your budget calls for. What do they do? They show you a model that doesn't have all the options that you want, but has enough of them. It's less than the car you really liked. You say, "Maybe I can squeeze a few more dollars or add a few more dollars to the budget." You end up buying that car.

What happened? You were misdirected. You walked in with a certain budget. The car dealer knew if he showed you this luxury top-of-the-line vehicle and the price was close enough he would direct your attention from that smaller vehicle back to the larger vehicle. You ended up paying more than you wanted to. This is how misdirection occurs. To combat this strategy in a negotiation, you might say, "I can't afford the vehicle I want so I'm not going to buy one today." Then, get up and begin to walk away. Take note of the action that follows. Does the car dealer do something to keep you engaged in the process? If he does, you've turned his attempts to misdirect you against him, which means at that point you are in a power position.

Savvy negotiators will label misdirection. If you have been misdirected to your detriment, you can call it what it is by stating to the other negotiator something such as:

- ▶ "That was nice what you just did."
- ▶ "What do you mean?"
- ▶ "You attempted to misdirect me from the point that we were really talking about. I applaud you for the strategy you tried to implement, but now let's get back to. . . ."

Then you move back to the position that you were asserting before the misdirection took place. What have you done with that situation? You misdirected the other negotiator by directing attention back to the topic. Be aware when misdirection attempts are being made and why they're being made, when they're being implemented or attempted to be implemented in relation to the goal.

LEADING THE BULLY

Lead the bully by the words that you choose. Say such things as, "I know you can see things from a better perspective if we adopt position X." The bully says, "I can see that might work." By emphasizing a visual perspective, the bully repeats it. That's a form of leading someone.

Contrast that to what happens if you say, "I can see a way out of the situation if we do X." The bully says, "That doesn't sound right to me." You now know you have more work to do to lead the bully. These are verbal clues you can insert into the dialogue when negotiating with a bully to see how successful you are in leading him. The feedback will let you know how successful you might be.

Use body language along with your words. Couple a gesture with your words. For example, you might also say something when you are speaking such as, "What would be your best scenario to work this situation out?" Touch the bully on his hand for just a few seconds. If the bully does not withdraw his hand when you touch it, the bully is communicating through the nonverbal gesture that he is willing to at least consider what you're saying.

The bully's response lets you know you are beginning to lead him. If you continue to pose such questions and he responds by smiling as you're offering solutions, that can give you more insight. You would be on the path of leading him.

LEADING FROM BEHIND

Leading from behind can be used to allow others to put forth their thoughts to see how they will be implemented. At the same time, you're assisting them by not only adopting what they say to a point when it serves your purpose. This allows them to believe they are in charge during the negotiation. During one of my media interviews, I spoke about how President Obama negotiated with the U.S. Congress on the healthcare bill. The question the interviewer asked me was, "Do you think the president leading from behind is a good strategy?" (He allowed Congress to take the lead.) I said, "Yes, it can be depending upon your overall strategy."

Those are some of the ways you can determine if you are being successful in leading a bully, while at the same time allowing him to think he's really the one who is leading the negotiation.

Leading from behind may be perceived as trying to trick someone. Be mindful of the words you choose so that the bully does not perceive you are being deceitful when you're trying to either lead the bully or get the bully to alter his perspective.

For example, if you really want a bully to eat chocolate ice cream you would say, "You don't want the chocolate ice cream. Chocolate ice cream is bad for you. Man, the chocolate ice cream is going to have all kinds of negative effects on you." Knowing the bully is unwilling to take any advice from you, the bully may demand chocolate ice cream. The chocolate ice cream is what you want the bully to accept. Chocolate ice cream can be a metaphor for anything in a negotiation you would want the bully to agree to while knowing if you say "A" the bully is going to say "B." If you say "night," the bully is going to say "day."

In a negotiation, ploys can be used to show something doesn't have a lot of value to you. Or you want to elevate its value in the eyes of the bully. These are "red herrings" in negotiations. You give something more value than it has as a pretense to make the bully think it's worth more.

WORD CHOICE IS CRUCIAL

You not only impact the bully's behavior by your words, but you also lead the bully at the same time. Be very mindful of the words you choose to use. "This is good for you" is stronger than "This is okay for you." Even your word choices can determine how a bully is going to not only perceive what you're offering in a negotiation but how likely it is that he will see your offers as beneficial.

These strategies need to be taken into consideration when you're talking to a bully and trying to lead him through your words. Carefully consider the best words to use; the bully will associate different outcomes with your choices. Thinking through the way you will speak with the bully is part of your planning stage, way before you get into the negotiation with the bully. Observing the bully in different environments gives you clues as to which strategy is best to use against him when you sit down and start to negotiate with him.

Sometimes you have prior knowledge about the bully's behavior and sometimes you're caught up in the moment, like the previous example of a person who accidentally cut into a line. Getting the bully to follow your lead in a negotiation can make all the difference in your success.

The reason it's so important that you are aware if the bully is following your lead or not is because your next step in your strategy is dependent upon the bully doing what you have asked of him.

Make sure the bully is following your lead in adopting the right strategy to continue from that point in the negotiation. In the best-case scenario, the bully accepts your lead and you reach a satisfactory conclusion to your negotiation. We know because of the way the bully's personality is wired he could be fighting against your tactics. What do you have to be concerned about if that occurs? If the bully is fighting against your tactics, it may be time to either call a time out or ask the bully, "What is it that you really want to occur out of this particular situation?" The bully then gives you his perspective of what he really wants.

Here's where misdirection can also come into play. You can say, "I can't do that." The bully replies, "In order for this deal to conclude successfully from my perspective I must have a million dollars." You can say to the bully, "I don't have a million dollars. There's no way in the world I can come up with a million dollars."

If the bully is just testing to see if you could come up with a million dollars what you need to do is have that bully understand there's no way it is going to occur. You could say something to the effect of, "Let's be more realistic." If you position the bully from that perspective, then the bully can show you there's no need for you to fight the million-dollar tactic anymore. This was the strategy the FBI employed years ago when U.S. citizens were kidnapped in South America. They repositioned the expectations before the kidnappers thought the official negotiation had begun.

Suppose the bully acquiesces and says, "Okay, let's talk about $500,000." You know the bully is becoming more reasonable. If the bully maintains he's going to stick to that million-dollar demand, it's time to exit the negotiation. You show you are not willing to negotiate; his tactic will not work. Just by showing you are ready to walk away may be effective in showing the bully you're fighting against his demands.

Based on what you have already gathered about the bully, you have learned he needs to make a deal. You've discovered what he is seeking, and you have gained insight about his timeframe for needing to conclude the deal. This knowledge gives you some leverage. Your threat to walk away provides some misdirection. But be careful as to how much insight you give the bully because in some cases the more you feed the beast the bigger the beast becomes.

SQUASHING BULLYING BEHAVIOR AT WORK

Consider the situation of the employee who is being bullied at work. Suppose the bully is the boss. The employee is in a vulnerable, subordinate position, which encourages the bully. In corporations, human resource departments provide the employee with backup. It is their role to step in when there is an unpleasant environment being created by a bully because of sexual innuendos, sexual harassment, racist remarks, insults about an employees' sexual orientation, religion, or other factors.

We have seen such incidents occur in companies, such as the media and TV networks. There was one man who was a major star at a TV network. He constantly harassed women to the point the women started sharing their stories. You would think this would be the end of the behavior, but the TV networks did not act and failed those employees who complained about the bullying. Eventually the situation got so out of hand that the owners of the station stepped in. They ended up firing the TV star and that was how the problem was solved.

Seek leverage in situations where you're not strong enough as an individual to combat the bully. My perspective is: Because you're always negotiating you can find resources, if the time and effort is worth it, to combat anyone who is bullying you.

The bully may perceive he has leverage against his target. "If you report this incident, I will write you up as a poor performer and that will affect your success at this company." Leverage turns to threats and blackmail when it is used in such a coercive manner. In this sense the bully uses blackmail to silence the target. It is a dirty trick that can backfire.

In one case, a senator was threatened with blackmail if he did not agree to be involved in blackmailing someone else. To not allow the blackmail attempts to occur, the senator let the story out himself and he exposed the other person. That individual ended up going to jail. By not agreeing to the blackmail activities, the senator took the leverage away from his blackmailer and used that against the individual. You must be cautious when you're using this type of leverage, and to what degree these repercussions may backfire on you.

ROLE-PLAYING AND THE BULLY'S POWER

It is so important to understand the support system the bully has because you can then understand the bully's real power. If that support is weak it will dissolve. If you show enough backbone with enough backed force, his backing will dissolve, and you know you can use that as a strategy to make a bully's support group wither. You have more insight for a negotiation.

In preparation for fighting back, role-playing will enable you to practice the strategies you will use to manipulate the bully to adopt one action versus another. If you understand how she gathered power, you have more knowledge as to how you can take power away from her or use the bully's power source against her.

A bully could lose power, a dynamic that influences how you role-play to develop strategies to help you succeed in a negotiation to remove the bully's power and add to your own.

History provides more lessons on a bully's power ploys. During World War II, Italian dictator Benito Mussolini lost his power base. People turned against him because they were losing the war. He ended up being executed. As the Soviets closed in on Berlin, Adolf Hitler received news of Mussolini's death. Determined not to let his enemies kill him, Hitler committed suicide after making arrangements for his corpse to be burned.[3]

If you understand how bullies have lost power in the past you can utilize some of the strategies that caused them to lose power in your role-play situations and thus you test different theories. Look at "what if" scenarios based on historical perspectives to gain more insight about how you can utilize those tactics. You examine, hone, and then determine how you're going to implement those in your role-playing situations.

For example, think about how you can convey strength and power in your role-playing. Seek ways to uncover thoughts or ideas you had not considered in your role-playing based on historical perspectives of how to implement tactics to thwart a bully's efforts.

Consider how you can divide and conquer the bully and his team as the result of placing wedges between them. Find out who really wants what by gathering information. Probe to determine why somebody is negotiating in the team and how you can turn them into an ally. That's what the spy game is all about—finding out what someone's real needs are. If you can do that, you can also think of ways you might be able to deny the bully attention he might want.

Remember to speak the bully's language. If a bully says, "I'm going to kick your butt," you don't want to say, "If you happen to raise your foot toward that part of my anatomy, I'm going to smack you across the face." You're not talking tough language in response to a bully saying, "I'm going to kick your butt." Use the language the bully understands.

Role-playing allows you to prepare for a bully's reactions to your efforts to thwart him and use strategies to address his actions. Always consider wedge issues in your role-playing scenarios. The best way to uncover those is to know as much about how a bully came to power, how he might lose the power, and insert those into your role-playing exercises as much as you possibly can.

In Conclusion

When it comes to negotiating with a bully, be observant ahead of your negotiation. Gather as much information as possible so you can predict how the bully will react in certain situations and how the bully thinks. Consider why he acts the way he does, who supports him, what would allow him to deescalate a situation, and the best time to negotiate with him.

You have a greater chance of winning the negotiation when you analyze those factors. In understanding what is most important to the bully, you know what you can use as possible leverage, what you should stay away from, or what it is the bully truly wants to accomplish.

Increase your skill in using negotiation strategies with the tips I provide on my website at this link: *http://themasternegotiator.com/negotiating-with-a-bully.*

Homework

Go back in history to any point (business, personal, political) and note how a bully came to power. Identify the allied forces he gathered and how he did so, the strategies he employed to gain more power, and what countermeasures overcame his power. Engaging in this exercise will give you better insight into how to deal with bullies at the negotiation table and in life.

4

Targeting the Vulnerable in the Workplace

Suppose you are at a point where you are ready to start a business or change careers. Consider your personality type. Is it competitive? Or are you non-confrontational? Because the skills you possess may fit across different industries, which industry might be best for you?

Different industries are rife with bullying. Being aware of these dynamics makes you better prepared to stand your ground. This chapter gives insight about the bullying maneuvers that occur in law enforcement, professional sports, gaming/casinos, TV broadcast news (especially female anchors), government, and large corporations. This knowledge will help you to be more selective about where you spend your time and the value you place on it. Because each of these areas also have individual variations as to how and why bullying occurs, having this awareness will allow you to better develop coping strategies.

WHY CORPORATIONS AND INDUSTRIES ARE RIPE FOR BULLYING

The culture of an industry will influence the degree to which bullying flourishes. Two good examples are the TV/movie industry and law enforcement. In the TV/movie industry, if you're going to be in front of the camera, you must be attractive. If those in charge don't perceive you as such, you can be bullied in the sense that they don't see your value as high as those who are considered attractive. How you look will determine how you are treated.

In the law enforcement industry, it was thought for many years that women could not perform in this environment simply because they did not have the physical requirements to do so. Those who set the standards also used people's ethnicity to bully them. When certain ethnicities arrived in the United States, stereotypes about their characteristics were developed.

As an example, African-Americans were viewed as lazy. In contrast to this prejudice, let's look at the situation in the northern part of the United States, Boston in particular. Here, a lot of the police officers were Irish immigrants. They obtained employment in an environment that was already full of like-minded people.[1]

Positions were made available for them, and it was relatively easy for them to rise through the ranks. In short, this work environment and culture allowed people to fall into a culture that had already been seeded for them to step into. This ease of absorption became more systemic with the progression of time.

In contrast, black people were not only unwelcome as police officers but were often their targets. Recently a white police officer was captured on video talking to a white individual whom he had pulled over. The white individual asked, "Well, you're not going to shoot me, are you?" The white police officer said, "No. Haven't you been watching TV? We only do that to black people."[2]

Think about that perspective. The mindset of that individual is more than likely systemic within his department. His bias sets him up to address someone who is non-Caucasian in a specific manner.

It's exactly that kind of systemic programming that makes some industries riper for bullying than others.

It Can Happen in Any Industry

The dominant culture of an industry or corporation might not have values that support bullying, but that doesn't mean bullying won't happen.

An Indian woman who had a highly placed position in a small company went to her manager after she had accepted additional responsibilities. She realized she was working nine to ten hours a day and not getting time for lunch. No one else in the company was working those long hours or having to give up their meal time. She asked her manager for one of the responsibilities to be removed from her load so she could concentrate on a project that the company had prioritized.

Instead of her manager applauding her demanding work, her initiative, and her creative effort to develop this new project, he attacked her personally and expressed dissatisfaction with her performance. He had never negatively evaluated her before.

She was amazed by his reaction and was so dismayed that she decided to resign on the spot. She has since learned that her responsibilities were spread among ten people within the company. Her manager saved money by not replacing her position, which made her wonder if he had a financial incentive to force her out of her job.

It's possible that ethnic prejudice also fueled this bullying. The woman noted that the manager looked surprised when she stood up for herself. He probably believed a stereotypical perspective that Indian women are more docile than women of other ethnicities. He may have thought, "I can do this to her, and she's not going to stand up to me. If she does, it will be in such a mild form that I won't have any problems dealing with it at all."

Bullying as a Way of Life

Within industries known for bullying, some specific companies and sub-industries stand out. The professional sports industry is a good example, specifically football.

Once again, we find bullying associated with racism. For years, a belief was prevalent that African-Americans did not have the mental capacity to play the position of quarterback. Physicist William Shockley stirred up trouble when he said on television, "My research leads me inescapably to the opinion that the major cause of the American Negro's intellectual and social deficits is hereditary and racially genetic in origin and, thus, not remediable to a major degree by practical improvements in the environment." Expressing his views damaged his reputation.[3]

Successfully playing professional sports means keeping track of many aspects of the game. A lot is always going on at once. Many years passed before the first African-American was given the quarterback position, and even then, it was considered a novelty, some type of experiment, or a way to gain more attendance for a game.

This is characteristic of the environments in multiple industries in which the culture generates stereotyped thought processes about some ethnicities. It will cause those who are in power positions to look at those particular ethnicities through a filter of prejudice that prevents them from seeing people as individuals. They then decide their prejudiced and limited judgments permit them to act like bullies. Sometimes, they don't realize that they are fulfilling their confirmation biases (that is, looking for confirmations to match their perception of how things are).

You will find this kind of prejudice in the TV industry, the movie industry, law enforcement, and almost any corporate or industrial environment. Those who are the "wrong" race or gender can get stuck in the lower echelons of the business. The same prejudice that put the people in lower-ranking positions also keeps them there. That becomes a form of bullying that prevents people from rising to heights they otherwise could achieve.

BULLYING AND DYSFUNCTIONAL ENVIRONMENTS

We also need to be very aware and evaluate an industry's potential for having an environment of bullying. We see clear examples of this in large corporations. Dysfunctional environments get set up in which doing something wrong, whether it is illegal, bullying, or sexual harassment, is so ingrained in people's behavior that it becomes the norm. As of this writing, Congress has nondisclosure agreements about sexual harassment. These are put in place to prevent victims from bringing to light the wrongs that have been thrust upon them by those who occupy congressional seats. Worse, in some cases, taxpayers' money has been used to settle claims. Such occurrences lend validity to the actions of the perpetrators because they are shielded from the public.

Because it's the norm, it's now the new normal, and it's the way people are trained to function in that environment. You will often find environments in which an organization becomes dysfunctional. For example, there is a well-known bank whose employees were creating accounts for people who had not given permission to do so. The employees were rewarded for how many new accounts they could create, and if they did not go along with this plan, they were threatened with being fired.

In terms of how dishonesty, prejudice, and bullying become part of the "new normal," I'm reminded of *The Emperor's New Clothes* by Hans Christian Andersen. The emperor was parading around naked, but everybody was convinced that he was wearing beautiful finery until a child said, "But he does not have on any clothes." The emperor shuddered, for he knew that the child was right, but he thought, "The procession must go on!" He carried himself even more proudly, and the chamberlains walked along behind carrying the train that wasn't there.[4]

Like the emperor, the person or people at the top of an industry or the top of a corporation will set the standards for how others will act.

You can see what's going on in President Trump's White House. It is easy to recognize exactly how he has people jousting with one another to gain favor with him. We had a press secretary in that administration who was fired simply because he would not fight back strongly enough to show that he had the courage to do so.

ANALYZE A WORK CULTURE BEFORE JOINING IT

Whether you're considering a new job in your current field or changing careers, you'll need to look carefully at both the general environment and the specific dynamics of your future workplace. This will help you address how you might become part of it in a way that will keep you from becoming a target of bullying.

I'll go deeper into this later in the chapter, but some points are worth saying more than once. You must be very much aware of why bullying occurs and from what source it originates. It is best you avoid a job if bulling is coming from the top, especially if you're not the type of individual to be combatant or if you don't possess the characteristics or traits that are associated with that environment. Otherwise, you could be setting yourself up for a very bad outcome.

If you were a job applicant considering employment in one of the industries that we're discussing, you would want to know of any warning signs in advance that someone in the organization is an oppressor who's taking advantage of the people who are vulnerable. Here are some ways you can do that.

There are certain TV news organizations that have been in the news because of lawsuits filed in response to bullying that went on in those networks. You can assess the risks of working for such organizations by talking to people at social gatherings and networking organizations who are employed in that environment. They can give you inside information to confirm or rebut your suspicions.

You can look on the Internet. You can talk to associates. In today's networking environment it is so easy to find such information by making inquiries via social media and by finding the people who know what's occurring in real life.

You want an environment that will allow you to perform in the way that meets your standards and a way of working that enables you to reach your goals sooner rather than later. Bullying may prevent you from achieving these goals; an invisible hand may be ready to hold you back. You should do due diligence before entering the environment to find out if these kinds of obstacles exist.

Let's take that a step further. Say you have suspicions that there are some types of bullying tactics going on, even of a mild variety. (I say "mild" because in some environments people don't consider themselves to be bullies. They call themselves hard-nosed.) You may have a specific definition associated with the word "bullying" that differs from another person's definition. However, the outcome is still the same, and you need to know that.

Even if you strongly suspect the environment you're going into has a prevalence for bullying, you still need to verify the degree to which bullying occurs, with whom it occurs, when it occurs, and why it occurs. The reason it's so important to gather comprehensive data and to dig deeply is that bullying doesn't always result from the standard sources of ethnic or gender prejudice. You may not fall into the category of those who are bullied for those reasons.

You may be a male who is in excellent shape and someone who would be respected as a law enforcement officer. Even though there's systemic bullying occurring in that environment, you will not fall prey to it because you do not have the characteristics of the bully's target. You still must make sure you not only know about the environment that you're going into but at the same time understand why bullying occurs in that environment and to whom it occurs.

OTHER REASONS WHY PEOPLE ARE BULLIED

I've talked about ethnicities, about people who are black, Indian, and other nationalities who might be in a minority position in a culture. Another significant factor may be body appearance. I mentioned earlier that in the TV and movie industry, if you're in front of the camera, you need to be considered attractive. The industry has other physical standards that can be used as justification for bullying.

You could audition for a role that requires someone of hefty body size. If you fit the stereotype in this case, you will not be bullied. If you do not fit the stereotype of someone in that situation, for example, because you're thin, you possibly could be bullied simply because someone can say, "Why the heck would you show up for a position like this? Don't you know what we're looking for? Get out of here." You must understand the way people talk to you.

You also need to comprehend the body perspective someone has of anyone who's a candidate for bullying and the extent to which you may fit into that perception. Take into consideration also why it is that they think you are too fat, too thin, and so on in relation to how they look and how they see themselves. You will also want to consider the extent to which competitiveness enters the picture.

In a situation in which you're vying for a position that requires someone to be thin in a movie or on TV, another thin person might want to bully you also. She has the same body style as you do, and she's afraid that you might get the part instead of her. She may surreptitiously try to do something to you (which is another form of bullying) to make sure that she gets the part instead of you.

Other assumptions go into the perspective that leads to bullying based on body dimensions. We may assume someone who is overweight is out of shape and in poor health. They may be in better health than someone who is thin. It goes right back to how we interpret what we see: somebody fat, thin, out of shape, and so on.

We make assumptions instantly about someone's worth based on their physical appearance. Someone who is overweight might be considered not only out of shape but at the same time not a good worker. We also know certain ethnicities tend to look at other ethnicities as not being able to perform in certain environments. We also know statistically that people who are taller tend to make more money than people who are shorter.[4] People who are perceived as better looking tend to make more money than those who are not as good looking.

The perception of body style in diverse cultures plays a part in how people are perceived. In the Hawaiian culture, the heavier a person is, the more he or she is seen as having great worth. The United States and other Western cultures think the opposite way.

India provides a good example of this. When the husband of a friend of mine was growing up in India, the obese people were considered to be more powerful. They had the resources to be able to eat more than other people and therefore being overweight gave a person high status.

In contrast, when I was a kid playing baseball, the guys who were perceived to be overweight were seen as not being as good even if they could hit the ball better. Maybe they had some power they could use to hit a ball farther than some of the people who were not as big, but they were not as agile in the field and thus they weren't considered as good. Most of this kind of thinking came from the kids who were thin. Having that thought allowed the thinner kids to see themselves as possessing more value.

In all of these situations, the perception was mainly based on the reality of the geographical location that the people were in. That's why you always need to take into consideration the norms of the environment as an additional clue about how bullying may be expressed.

Body Types That Can Prevent Bullying

Regardless of the culture or environment in which you find yourself, it's very important not to be perceived as being weak. Bullies will tend to pick on whomever they perceive to be the weakest in the crowd. This tendency isn't limited to humans. Although we don't call it bullying, animals also attack the weakest.

When they are thinking about picking out their prey from a herd, predators will identify what they perceive as the weakest animal: the crippled, the smallest, or the youngest. The predator is looking for food, and it chooses the likeliest way to obtain it.

Humans use comparable selection methods. If they perceive someone as being too strong to combat, they will go after the least aggressive prey. If you walk around like you are an easy target, that's how they will identify you.

You must be very conscious of your body style. Whether you're short or tall, don't walk hunched over. Walk with a gait that says you're on the move and you're going someplace. Speak with authority even when you're speaking to those who are in a superior position, like a boss or superintendent.

Display respect, but don't allow yourself to be caught up in an environment in which you need to subjugate yourself. While being respectful, also act in a way that signals you are not subservient to someone simply because he or she is the "authority." Your attitude says, "I respect you, but at the same time I am not going to fall prey to you."

Regarding the story about the Indian woman who resigned after she was bullied, she could have set boundaries ahead of time to say, "Okay, I'll do this but . . ." People should always be aware of this important negotiation strategy. Look a situation as having an end point, and you need to decide what you want that end to be. Convey it before you enter the environment in a way that sets the expectations of the person with whom you're speaking.

Had the woman said to her boss, "The most I can do is probably an extra four hours every two weeks" or whatever number suited her best, she would have set his expectations. He would have then known that he would get X number of hours out of her. She could have avoided the inevitability of having to quit her job and could probably have prevented him from bullying her.

Always set expectations to prevent bullying. You do that by how you carry yourself and the way in which you present yourself. Body gestures have a true meaning in the way that you're perceived, so think about making strong body gestures. Walk with your head held high and your shoulders back. This projects energy and confidence. Keep your weight evenly distributed on your feet when you stand still. Place your hands on your hips when appropriate; when people take up more space they dominate a space.

Never slouch. When you look someone in the eyes, do so for an appropriate length of time. This does depend on the culture. In some cultures, if you look someone in the eye for five or ten seconds, that could be considered an invitation to a fight. People think, "What are you staring at?" In these kinds of cultures, you keep your eyes lowered because that says "I'm being respectful." If you feel uncomfortable looking people in the eye, look at their nose. From their perspective it will appear that you are still looking them in the eye.

You need to keep many considerations in mind when you're using your body to convey the fact that you're respectful and at the same time not a target. Conveying respect without submission, adopting a purposeful posture, and avoiding the appearance of weakness are valuable tools.

IDENTIFYING SUBTLE FORMS OF BULLYING

I've stated that bullying is sometimes overt and sometimes subtle. We all have value systems that allow us to rank others and ourselves in terms of a given hierarchy. No matter how good we think we are, we will judge some environments we're in as being more threatening. We need to have a toolbox of negotiation strategies.

If you're in an environment in which you know the value system may be against you simply because of how someone perceives your ethnicity, you can alter that by making sure you have leverage.

Once, when I was younger, I was purchasing an automobile. My evaluation of the situation was that if I went by myself, I would be perceived as not financially able to purchase the car. The car salesperson might try to negotiate with me more stringently than he otherwise would. I asked a Caucasian friend of mine to go in and help me purchase the car.

In this situation, my expectations were realized. Even though I stated that I was the purchaser, the car salesperson kept looking at my friend for answers to questions.

We ended up getting a deal that I was happy with, but I suspected that because I am African-American I would not have gotten as good of a deal had my friend not been with me. The salesperson's perspective included prejudices against the buying power of a young African-American.

This sort of prejudice can be used against even obviously rich African-Americans, such as hip-hop artists. Some of them have much more money than the car dealership has, let alone the car salesperson. However, in the past they would go in to buy a car, and initially, car salesmen did not even want to deal with them. Someone who has a stereotyped perception of you based on your identification as a racial or ethnic "type" and doesn't want to deal with you is practicing a form of bullying.

I had a similar experience when I was working with two well-known seminar leaders. We were doing back-of-the-room sales, and a woman in her late twenties or early thirties came in. We were selling big-ticket items, which in this instance meant items in the range of $10,000 to $20,000. We were also working partially on commission.

I went over toward the woman after several of my colleagues had neglected her. She and I started talking, and she ended up pulling out an Black Centurion American Express Card. She made a $75,000 purchase.

Although I overcame my prejudice that she didn't have enough money to be worth my time, I admit that I, along with my colleagues, expressed some other biases about her. We started wondering how this woman could afford to have and freely use an American Express Black Card. We weren't even prepared to consider the possibility that she was a powerful and successful woman in her own right. To this day I'm remorseful for having once thought like that, but I grew from that experience.

NEGOTIATION STRATEGIES

By now, you realize in how many ways, both blatant and subtle, bullying can be expressed. Having the ability to identify bullying represents the first stage of empowerment. Let's move on to the action stage.

How can you assess the kinds of negotiation strategies that work best in certain industries and corporate environments? The first thing to realize is that no one strategy will fit every situation. Situations are flexible and fluid, and you need to read them carefully and adapt your response accordingly. Remember: You're always negotiating, so even before you enter an environment, you need to know what you might be confronted with to adopt strategies.

Let's say that you know you're in an environment that has an extremely strong culture of folks bullying other individuals. Some people adopt strategies wherein they either position themselves as someone to be reckoned with, someone not to be deflected by diversionary tactics, or someone who says, "If you try to get me, I'm going to come at you twice as hard."

Remember these are choices of tactics. You should always present an image of strength and awareness, but projecting a menacing attitude changes the dynamics.

If you know the person who's doing the bullying is in a weakened position, you can call upon others as leverage to support your efforts and combat him. This involves a thorough evaluation of the situation and great caution. You may have heard the cliché, "He who fights and runs away lives to fight another day."

In some cases, the proper negotiation strategy may be to simply retreat. However, if you use this strategy, do so while still presenting the image of someone who's only retreating for a moment. This leaves open the option that you can return at a moment's notice if the other person comes after you.

Simply put, you project this message: "Leave me alone for right now, and everything will be fine. If you come after me, though, you may have hell to pay."

We've seen a vivid example of this in the situation with North Korea. When they fired off their hydrogen bomb, the United States asked for assistance from China and Russia. Most people may perceive North Korea as being a bully. China does not perceive North Korea in this way because, from their perspective, North Korea is an annex of China. Plus, China sees North Korea as a buffer between it and the U.S. ally of South Korea. When considering how you might use a bully's ally against him, take into consideration what the ally seeks from the bully.

The U.S. sought assistance from both China and Russia for leverage in this situation to combat North Korea. At the same time, North Korea was constantly verbally poking the United States. Eventually the negotiation strategy of using leverage from China and Russia to combat North Korea could lose its effectiveness.

The different strategies being utilized depend upon the environment as it exists in any moment. You can be tough when toughness is required, but think about the price you might later have to pay for your toughness. You can be meek. You can be mild.

Think about whatever action you adopt in the form of a negotiation strategy. Think about what that action will lead to because you engaged in it today and how it will position you for future actions and/or bullying tomorrow.

BEWARE OF BLOWBACK

Failure to consider the short- and long-term consequences can cause retaliation, often called a "blowback" effect. The following examples illustrate this.

As the union steward of a restaurant union, Alice had a brainstorm. She said to an associate, "Let's see what we can do to increase the pressure on management to agree to our demands for improved benefits. We can talk to some of our customers and persuade them to stop coming to the restaurant. That will slow the cash flow and make management really listen to us."

Alice and her associate devised a plan to visit customers at their homes and businesses to encourage them to boycott the restaurant. Their actions led to a federal lawsuit accusing the union of harassing customers.

A woman in the food service industry was working for a man who was from another culture. He had the habit of putting his hands on her in inappropriate places. She was raised to believe that she was in control of her own body and that nobody should have wandering hands without her permission. She was enraged by his behavior, and she correctly identified it as sexual harassment.

She applied for a transfer to another part of the company. Before the transfer had been granted, she filed a complaint about this man's behavior. As a result, she was fired from her position and was forced to leave and get a job in a situation that was not commensurate with the education that she had gone through to become a pastry chef.

She didn't think through the implication of filing the sexual harassment claim while waiting to get transferred. This is a prime example of blowback, or retaliation effect, that illustrates what can happen to the whistle-blower. She had a legitimate concern. It was valid, it was legal, but she didn't give enough thought about how to handle that situation in a way that would protect her.

In another situation involving sexual harassment, a woman filed a complaint against her supervisor, who had a pattern of backing her against a wall and feeling her breasts. The man tipped off the police that this woman might have drugs in her apartment. The police carried out a raid and found cash and drugs, both of which they confiscated. The value of the woman's case against her supervisor was greatly diminished by her arrest.

It doesn't matter if the law is on your side if you don't position yourself properly. You always need to consider how a situation is going to play out before you initiate action: what you can do and what the implications are for you if you don't play this out correctly.

I can't emphasize enough that you're always negotiating and what you do today influences tomorrow's results. Here's another example that reinforces this point.

I was at a table where a female blackjack dealer was working. I noticed that when the floor person—who was male—walked behind her, she would flinch for a moment. I finally realized that he was touching her inappropriately. I said to her, "Why don't you tell somebody about that?" She said, "Are you kidding? If I did, I would be black-listed from all the casinos."

Here we have an example of an industry that promotes bullying and forces female employees to either accept this injurious behavior being thrust upon them or lose their livelihood. This individual could move to a different state, but that might not prevent blowback.

A phrase to keep in mind about blowback is, "Revenge is a dish best served cold." You may do something to someone today and completely forget about it. It may have no meaning to you. The person to whom you did it, however, can lay plans for revenge. This could include preventing you from being promoted or getting the job you want.

The following examples of blowback are directed at well-known actors and actresses (whose names have been omitted). These anecdotes also remind us that bullying can jeopardize the most spectacular career.

▶ An actress already known for acting like a diva in her singing career got a very poor reputation in the movie world. People who worked with her claimed she had made endless demands on those associated with various productions and that she was known as a troublemaker. Eventually, many people from casts and crews refused to work with her.

▶ Another well-known actress also has a reputation for being demanding on film sets. She is also reported to treat cast members, film crews, and even fans with contempt.

▶ An actor is known for having anger issues and disruptive behavior. After he slapped a female co-star, he was banned from ever again performing on a popular television show.

▶ Another actor with anger management issues created an image so troublesome that many casting directors, producers, and movie industry officials refused to work with him.

Obsessive and controlling behavior has led to the demise of the careers of several actors. One actor refused to allow anything to happen on set without his approval. Another formerly very successful actor is now reduced to only action movies. A third, who claimed that a movie he called "bad" succeeded only because he was in it, is now rarely seen on screen.

THE VALUE OF TEAMWORK

You must be very much concerned about how you protect your rights or expose a wrong. Often, a situation requires larger forces to support your effort. Always consider this possibility and, when necessary, have others looking out for you.

Many years ago, a critical health situation developed in the Buffalo, New York, area. This centered on the pollution of a body of water called Love Canal. Both adults and children were developing serious illnesses from toxins seeping into their houses and from the drinking water. The corporation responsible for the toxic dumping denied that the wave of illness had anything to do with its actions.

One woman started fighting the system and attempts were made to shut her down. She was successful because she used the news media as leverage to bring the story to a larger audience. That was her source of protection as she went forward. Her opposition knew that if they came after her, she had a larger force waiting to combat them on her behalf.

She thought strategically. You must always do that and especially consider the results of your actions. Sometimes you need to delay action and instead gather more insight and information. Armed with facts, you can build your case and present it in a more persuasive manner to a larger audience who might be able to support your efforts. If you haven't created the basis for such an audience, action may not be possible.

This underscores the point that before you go into an environment, you should know what that environment is like. Know to what degree you may have to accept some abuse that doesn't exist in other settings. You may decide the possible benefits don't warrant the difficulties of trying to function in such a situation.

WHISTLEBLOWERS

Industries and agencies are aware of the risk of blowback. They have put in place, to varying degrees of success, whistleblower laws that protect people who speak up and who position themselves so that they can protect themselves.

From a legal perspective, there is something called "Qui Tam." This law makes provisions that the person who acts as the whistleblower and brings forth a complaint to the U.S. government is entitled to a percentage of the recovery. For example, whistleblowers may file lawsuits because they're aware of fraud in Medicare billing. If the government can get back $120 million of revenue, the whistleblower may be entitled to a percentage of that.[5]

For this reason, it can be very important to know the laws when it comes to whistleblowing. At the same time, being legally right doesn't guarantee protection from blowback, as the following story demonstrates.

A pathologist began helping hospitals recognize certain data patterns. His strong medical background helped him to understand data from a hospital that had four times the normal rate of a specific type of pneumonia. As a physician, he knew that it would be very unusual for hospitals to be taking care of patients with that type of pneumonia as opposed to a more ordinary form.

He discovered that the more exotic form of pneumonia brought much higher forms of reimbursement. Further investigation revealed that several other hospitals were incorrectly coding to increase their gain. He filed a Qui Tam motion and got back a large amount of money. But he was also told that if he went into the western part of his state, he would be in a lot of trouble. People were parking in his driveway and watching his actions because he had acted as a whistleblower.

Ultimately, he decided that he was not going to pursue any other cases of billing fraud. He had made his point, and he obtained money, but the cost to him in terms of personal safety was too high.

Another incident occurred many years ago in the New York City Police Department. At the time, the department members were extremely corrupt and taking payoffs. An officer named Frank Serpico refused to take bribes. During that time, he exposed the corruption in the police department. As a result, when he got into an altercation that required backup, his partners did not back him up. He was shot in the face by a heroin dealer. He realized that the message they were sending him was: "Okay you exposed us. We will not have your back." After that he retired.[6]

The doctor was scared away by threats. Serpico withdrew from his job after a blatant threat to his survival.

That's why deciding to be a whistleblower is such a tough decision. Sometimes you may decide that the potential price to pay is too high. You might step back, hoping that someone else will do it. On the other hand, you may decide to let your conscience be your guide.

Whistleblowing can have a powerful effect. Minorities in some states claimed that they were pulled over or stopped more frequently while driving than non-minorities. Non-minorities, especially those in the police department, claimed that this was untrue.

In several different states, including New Jersey, Maryland, Ohio, and Illinois, police officers routinely pull over African-American drivers at rates far more than their presence as traffic code offenders on our nation's highways. A survey of the empirical literature suggests that minority drivers are three times more likely to be searched during a traffic stop than Caucasian drivers, and nonracial cues cannot explain this disparity. Currently, the Civil Rights Division of the U.S. Department of Justice and more than half of all states monitor racial profiling.[7]

The confirmation of this racism highlighted a type of bullying. Had the light not been shone upon it, the police stops would have more than likely continued until something even more drastic occurred to change it. That's what needs to be done in a bullying environment. Something needs to occur that is so drastic that the discrepancies that are part of the bullying characteristics are displayed in front of all to see. Only then will positive change take place.

UNDERSTANDING WHY PEOPLE ARE BULLIES

You can find bullies in all socioeconomic classes, from the poorest person to the richest. Family and corporate values support, endorse, and teach bullying behavior to people.

Take the situation of a person who grows up in a gang. The gang requires adherence to rules, with well-defined turf lines, tattoos, hand signals, and initiation procedures that often involve violent crimes. People living in a neighborhood with gangs need to understand the gang members' behavior; this knowledge is essential for their own self-preservation.

As another example, there are corporate cultures that dictate tough negotiation behavior. You would use a host of negotiation strategies if you were dealing with a person whose ingrained behavior is based on corporate norms of bullying. Let's say the corporate culture centers on a perspective of "I win, you lose." You would adopt different strategies with that person, making sure you're not in a position that means the only way you can get the agreement is to sell your soul.

Before you can conquer a bully, you must know how he thinks. Part of understanding that process means knowing as much as possible about the bully's current environment. This encompasses his home, work, and leisure environments. He may be stimulated to act a certain way based on the associates he has in those environments. If you understand what makes him tick, you'll be better prepared to confront him.

In some situations, you will be able to glean insight into the bully's values by observing those with whom he associates. Seek to understand the values his closest associates have and which he endorses. He will follow their lead because, to fit into that group, he must uphold the group's value system. Otherwise, the group won't accept him. Once you're aware of a bully's environment and his mindset, you can best determine the strategy to use in your attempts to get him to back off.

Bullying develops because of life experiences. A person may start off in life as someone who is gentle, kind, and giving. In some situations, family values teach the child to be hard-nosed and ruthless. Closing the deal in his favor *by any means necessary* will be the most important value in the family. This child will become conditioned to use strategies designed to win.

In a more cooperative environment, people learn to behave differently. Today's children have a more global perspective. They may be playing computer games with other individuals on the opposite side of the earth. They are learning to erase boundaries and create new understandings with people from other cultures. This means that if you're negotiating with a younger person, you may reasonably anticipate a more cooperative approach to negotiation.

You'll often find people make certain assumptions to bolster their self-esteem. It doesn't matter if these assumptions have nothing to do with reality. Their importance lies in the degree to which people comfort themselves about where they are in life or try to fill in the blank regarding how someone could have gotten so much more than they believe they have in their lives. People may bully those they see as "having more" until they have a better understanding of reality. This could be the antidote to bullying.

In trying to understand why people bully others, ask yourself if they're insecure and trying to make themselves feel better.

An outstanding example of this is President Donald Trump. If you pay attention to the language he uses, you'll gain insight into the fact that he is not very well versed on current situations and environments. This may be why he has a bullying attitude that he projects upon others. It's a way to insulate himself from his lack of knowledge.

Some of those who use such bullying tactics do so as a form of protection. The reasoning probably goes something like this: "You can't attack me for my lack of knowledge while I'm attacking you for whatever haphazard reason I may throw at you. While I'm doing so, you're not discovering the fact that I am inadequate or inefficient in some situations."

USING LEVERAGE TO PREVENT BULLYING

One method is to look at sources the bully admires, try to gain those sources as resources for you, and use that for leverage. Say that an associate of the bully—we'll call him Joe—has come to like you. The bully thinks, "Hey, Joe said he's okay. If Joe said that, I'd better leave him alone."

That's a form of leverage you can use as the result of the bully's respect for Joe. You really need to know what the bully is trying to achieve and to what degree others are supporting his efforts. You then find a way to use these facts to your advantage.

Knowing the bully's environment and source of motivation gives you insight as to what leverage you can use and then how to go about gaining such leverage. For example, would it position you best to appear as competition to the bully? That's one option. Another is for you to make those who support the bully believe you support him. These allies may then say to the bully, "Leave him alone. He's with us. He's supporting your efforts."

You may end up outperforming the bully. Then you're making the bully look bad to those who are supporting him. They thus will favor you over him, and that could prevent the bully from moving against you because you have greater protection now. At this point, though, you need to consider that the bully might do something behind your back.

All of those are points of consideration before actually engaging with the bully. Doing so addresses whatever he's doing that's causing you to feel less effective than you want to feel because of your interactions with him.

SUPPORT SYSTEMS

The support systems you try to align with to acquire leverage in bullying cultures depend on the environment. In the TV and movie industry, it might involve seeking the support of the sponsors. One news superstar constantly engaged in bullying practices with women. The network allowed it to occur because he was the star of the network. It wasn't until sponsors started pulling their commercials off that network that his behavior got the network's attention.

The overall leverage that led to the sponsors pulling out was the negative way the public viewed his behavior. The sponsors paid attention because those who bought their products were objecting to the star. Recognizing that a drop in sales could soon follow, they decided they did not wish to be associated with that individual and network. Public opinion leading to sponsors' boycotts of the network removed network support for this TV news star.[8]

Although the general environment you're dealing with is important, you're always looking for an entity who will have the greatest influence. We also need to consider that the bully perceives his actions as the use of power. Power is fluid; it can be strong at one time and weak at another moment. That next moment could be the time that the power has ebbed and flowed and has dissipated altogether. Think about the timing in terms of what leverage you will use and who will be the target.

Had the women who filed suit against this TV network news star gone to the public first, they might not have gotten the positive results that occurred when the public put pressure on the sponsors and the sponsors pulled.

Understand who is in the power position, who you can get on your side, and what you can use as leverage against the opponents. You can take that as deep as you need to so that you achieve the outcome that you're seeking.

BULLYING IN A NEGOTIATION

When you're involved in a negotiation, consider the mind games typically played by a hardcore negotiator. This person has already made up her mind how the negotiation is going to go. You are there just to sign the agreement that she has tilted in her favor. She asks, "Any questions? I don't think so. Here is where you sign." That could come across as bullying. Large corporations use that tactic at times.

Bullying can be demonstrated by the message, "I am so much bigger than you. You need me more than I need you." How do you confront something like that? First, you don't put yourself in that position. You're always negotiating, and thus you don't accept all your business from one corporation. You diversify.

Suppose you find yourself in a position where you really want the business. Don't have the mindset that if you don't get the business, the world ends. That mindset will put you in a position to be bullied. Bullying can take the form of someone who is overly aggressive, has a hidden agenda, or is extremely manipulative.

When I was the head of a subdivision, people who reported to me were supposed to turn in a report at a particular time. One person was consistently late turning in the report. I asked this individual to please get his report in, saying, "If you don't, our whole team is late in getting our report in." Yet he would not comply. One day I sent him an email. I copied the person who was the head of the group on the email. The delinquent employee accused me of being passive-aggressive, although that was not my intent.

You might be perceived as being a bully when your intent is different. If you are negotiating with a person whom you trust, ask him or her for verification. When you are clear on your intention and motivation, your strategy would vary based on the outcome you seek:

► "Here's what I think of your accusation." (Aggressive)

► "What is your intent in calling me passive-aggressive?" (Inquisitive)

► "I think calling me passive-aggressive is an attempt to divert attention away from your failure to produce your material on time. Let's talk about that behavior and my expectations of you as your manager." (Analytical)

ACKNOWLEDGMENT OF BULLYING

What do you do with the person who says, "Yes, I am trying to bully you or force you into accepting my terms?" Here is where positioning comes into play. Before you can enter the negotiation, you need to know what type of people you are going to be negotiating with. What are their favorite mind games? You go into the negotiation knowing you have back-door strategies. You might say, "I don't negotiate with bullies. When you choose to change your behavior, let me know." Get up to walk away and see what he does.

Avoid the risk of becoming too reliant on a client. Make sure you have other outlets through which you can obtain what you need and know how quickly you can obtain it. Knowing the timeliness of your client's needs also gives you leverage and governs how you react.

Be prepared to walk away from a deal with a bully. If you start to walk out of the room, and the bully stops you, he has revealed himself as being ready to negotiate. You can take the approach of "Let's see if we could do this together." You become a collaborative negotiator as opposed to a combative one.

IN CONCLUSION

When it comes to bullying, understand that the bully is going to take the course of least resistance. If you are not the course of least resistance, the bully will pass you over, and thus you always need to give the appearance of being strong. That strong appearance can come in many forms based on the industry and the corporation that you are in.

Understand the mindset of those who are in charge, the power people. Understand how they came to be in those power positions. Understand what they're seeking as outcomes to serve their clients. This will give you a road map of how to not only prevent being bullied but also how you can ingratiate yourself to the degree you start rising above others, even those who may be performing bullying tactics to trample others to achieve their goals.

I have additional resources for you on my website at this link: *http://themasternegotiator.com/negotiating-with-a-bully*.

HOMEWORK

If you are currently in the workforce take note of what is prevalent in the industry related to bullying and note the differences in your organization. Note why the differences occur, how they came about in your organization versus the industry, and the direction that both are headed in related to addressing the bullying that occurs. This exercise will allow you to become better prepared to utilize allies to combat potential bullying that may occur to you in the future.

If you are just entering the workforce or considering a change in your industry, note the influences that allow or curtail bullying in the industry you are thinking of moving into. How much tolerance do you have for bullying? Going through this exercise will give you insight into your possible viability and potential success in that industry as it relates to the potential bullying or aggression you may have to deal with to excel in that industry. To make a better assessment, appraise the company in which you will seek employment to determine where it stands on the bully scale. Based on your findings you will gain insight about the expectations you may have to engage in to become successful.

5

Costs: Pinpointing the Price of Bullying

There is a distinction between negotiating with a bully at school, home, or work. The differences center around the tactics that you adopt to deal with the bully in that environment. This chapter focuses on costs of bullying—both on the target and the bully. It includes firsthand perspectives of people who are familiar with bullies.

You can maximize the efforts of your negotiation tactics against the bully when you understand how he acts in a home environment where he may feel he has more dominance. In a work environment, he may behave differently because there may be a subordinate who is bullying him versus a school environment. He will display a different persona based on how he is seen and sees himself in that environment.

Consider how he perceives his bullying efforts. For example, a parent may consider spanking a child as a normal part of disciplining a child. Is this bullying? When does it go beyond discipline? Take into consideration the strategies that will best move him away from the behavior that you do not want him to display.

BULLYING AT HOME

In the home environment the bully may be a sister or a brother, an aunt or an uncle, a parent or a grandparent. A bully in a home often has great control over the target. As a person who was bullied as a kid, Brady Paterson, CEO of Success Road Academy in Vancouver, describes his stepfather as:

> [A]n incredible bully. On a daily basis it was constant bullying. He was telling me I was worthless, a piece a garbage. I was never going to be anything. That started from a very early age. He wasn't incredibly physically violent with me, but he was violent. I learned at home to protect my siblings and take the brunt of everything so that they could be safer from him. I turned into a punching bag at home.
>
> My stepfather one time said, "Do not call your mom" and I asked why. He had just moved in with us. My job was to get home from daycare, check on my siblings, and then call my mom. I called my mom and I promptly got caught, and promptly got a hell of a spanking after I got off the phone with her. He told me, "Don't ever tell your mom or I'll kill you" and not being able to tell my mom was not okay so I immediately told my mom.
>
> He didn't kill me. My mom of course said what he had told me was not okay. I made her promise not to tell him, but she immediately confronted him within minutes. The next time she wasn't around I got a hell of a licking and another death threat. It taught me that talking about it was bad because then I just got punished. I think we need to create a culture where we can talk about it and the punishment isn't happening. That would have made it a lot simpler and that would have made my life a lot easier.
>
> My mom after that thought the abuse stopped and she didn't know any better or at least until I was probably in my early teens or mid-teens. We had a six- to eight-year gap when I was still

getting continuing escalating abuse, but I was scared to tell her because the one time I told her it came back so much worse.

Get access to the full interview with Brady Paterson at *http://the-masternegotiator.com/negotiating-with-a-bully*.

In a company, the female partner found out about an egregious act her male partner performed: The male partner made a large deal without consulting with her. When the female partner referred to it during a fight, the male partner said, "I'm not going to take this anymore. We discussed this and it's over with." The female partner responded by saying, "But it's still hurting me." Her partner said, "I'll pack up my desk and I'll leave."

The threat of walking out the door was a bullying tactic. The tactic the partner was employing was a threat: "I'm going to shut you down by threatening to leave you. Now what do you think about that?"

If the situation is allowed to fester and the partner doesn't give up her grievance, the other partner's departure would cause loss of control of the negotiation. Always understand the level of control you want to maintain in any negotiation situation with a bully. In a home environment, the husband and wife both have a perspective of power. If one wants to usurp power by making a threatening gesture, it might be beneficial for the other individual to back down. "He who fights and runs away lives to fight another day." Remember the *way* you back down determines to what degree you will have to fight another day. When you fight/negotiate against a bully, you should do so on your own terms to the degree that you can.

When you're in a work environment, understand the dynamics that are occurring. Consider what led to that point and select the proper strategy. Consider the dynamics at work and how your current actions affect future interactions. Those who you are closest to understand you the most. They also realize how you think, which means they can know where your thoughts are heading and have a convincing rebuttal ready. You should be more introspective when negotiating with those who know how you think. Such individuals will have an advantage that is now available to others. That's another reason you should seek to under-stand how a bully thinks, and his motivations.

In the case of the man who threatened to walk out, the partner could have called the man's bluff, which would have escalated the situation be-cause now either he had to leave or be quiet. Suppose he said, "Wait, I am really committed to this business. I don't want to put you through such anguish again. If you would like me to leave, I will do so but I really don't want to." What does she say after that? "Okay, please stay." What he's done is given her power. Even bullies can relinquish power when it's appropriate for them to do so and the costs are too high to do otherwise.

BULLYING AT SCHOOL

Bullying in school encompasses students of all ages. There are differ-ences in the dynamics involving children up to the age of high school. These individuals have not matured to the degree of those in a work environment. The child has not grown into the level of knowledge that could otherwise allow him or her to reason a little better. This comes with maturity. Bullying in school can cause deep wounds that can last a lifetime.

Susan Binnie, a speaker, coach, and author who helps women write and share their stories to heal and prosper, describes what her daughter went through in school:

> She was bullied from fourth grade onward. In fourth grade, she was picked on in class and was told that she was no good. There were two girls who really would gang up on her. One would say, "Oh yeah, I'll be your partner and we've all got things worked out" and then the other one would also promise to be her part-ner. When it came time for them to partner up the teacher would say, "Have you guys all figured out your partners?" Then these two girls would say, "Yep we're partnering" and Caitlin would have nobody. They would laugh at her and make fun of her.
>
> Caitlin was always the one who was left out. After school, they would push her into her locker. They would call her names

and make fun of her. They would push her down on the floor and then say, "Oh look everyone. Look what Caitlin did. Look at how she fell on the floor" and just call a lot of attention to her.

We as parents went to the school to talk to them. We described these different scenarios of how she was picked on. They said, "We will have to talk to the other parents." We found out that one of the girls' moms was on the school board. Of course, they said, "It must have been Caitlin causing all the problems, so it must have been Caitlin's fault."

Caitlin's parents moved her into a different school system, where the pattern of bullying continued from a girl whose mother was also on the school board. Caitlin left school to complete her high school years on a home-schooling basis. Get access to the full interview with Susan Binnie at *http://themasternegotiator.com/negotiating-with-a-bully*.

When you're talking about someone in a school environment, you must be more mindful of how susceptible that person might be to peer pressure. You then must understand what strategies you would have to create for the person in the school environment.

Consider the developmental stage of children compared to where they should be; this explains their behavior. To the degree that you can, attempt to identify when the child's behavior patterns began to change; that will highlight the events that precipitated a change. You will get a beginning point for trying to alter or negotiate behavior change.

Here's the gist: Always know the mindset of the bully with whom you are negotiating or combating. Those words—"negotiating" and "combating"—take on different connotations based on how you perceive the individual and how the individual will perceive you.

Chuck Sutherland recalls his own encounters with bullying. Chuck is the owner of Sutherland Investments, which is involved in the construction, remodeling, ownership, and management of real estate properties. He also provides consulting and due diligence services for commercial real estate, residential, and industrial properties.

When I was in high school, and it all began in grade school, I was bullied a lot. It started in grade school, but it was mostly the same people. My winning formula in grade school and in high school was that I was smart. I studied and did well in school. In our high school, we had four different classes for the same subject we went through. There was what they called A, B, C, and D classes that related to grades. I was in the A class and the bullies were in mostly the C and D classes.

Even looking back today, I can't tell you why I was the victim. I've got some theories, but I would think people would have said I was weak because I wasn't strong and athletic.

When I was a junior in high school some of the kids threw all of my books out of the window of the bus. At a different time, the bus broke down, so the driver went to get help. There was a spare tire on the back of the bus, and so what they proceeded to do is pass it forward to hit me on the head with it, at which point I got off the bus. There wasn't anywhere nearby, but I just got off the bus and walked to a place where I could call my dad to come and get me.

That was a strategy I mostly used during that time. My dad gave me some advice about it, which I followed. He said, "You just go up to them and tell them that you're just going to beat the hell out of them. Whisper it in their ear that you're just going to beat the hell out of them if they don't leave you alone." I did that and got the hell beat out of *me*.

Get access to the full interview with Chuck Sutherland at *http://the-masternegotiator.com/negotiating-with-a-bully*. The lesson here is: Be prepared to back up your claims and actions. When negotiating, always be prepared for an action that may follow.

Kids bully other kids; teachers bully kids. It may be more common for a teacher to bully kids in lower levels of a school environment than the upper grades. In the upper grades, kids will start to literally fight the teacher back to regain some of his or her prominence.

In a teacher/student environment at younger levels of schools, parents need to tell the child what is proper behavior: "By the way, Junior, tell me if this does not occur in the environment." If it occurs, the child then knows there's a need to talk to parents.

Therein lies how a teacher who is bullying a kid can be addressed, but the kid must have the level of knowledge and insight to tell the parent. The parent then turns around and confronts the teacher. It is crucial to know how and when to use leverage in a negotiation. First, it starts with insights that lead to knowledge, which can transform into actions.

Bullying may also occur on the college level. One of my colleagues took a course taught by a very strict professor. He made it very clear that the students were not to enter his classroom late for any reason. If they couldn't be there at the time that he was ready to start, they were not allowed to come in after he began. He didn't want any distractions.

About fifteen minutes into his class one of my colleague's hard contact lenses shifted and it became extremely painful. She had tears pouring down her face and couldn't tolerate it. She got up and went to the ladies' room where she took the contact out, promptly dropped it on the floor, stepped on it, and that was end of the contact lens. When she walked back into the classroom without the contact lens, he stopped teaching and said, "You broke my rules. Now you have to come up and speak to me afterward."

When she spoke to him, she explained why she left. He told her she was going to have to write an extra paper for breaking the rules. At the beginning of the next class (they had taken a quiz in the meantime) he said, "Tell me what grade you got on your quiz." When she told him that she got an "A," he then said, "All right, I'll let you get by this time."

She felt like he was haranguing her over something, when he should have just said, "I understand your circumstances" and let it go.

You must understand a bully's demeanor. When you're in the bully's environment, you're dealing with his rules. To a degree, you must deal with him based on those rules. My colleague could have asked for permission to leave. When she got up without raising her hand, she was challenging the bully. If she asked for permission to leave, she would have positioned herself to avoid the rebuke and to convey "This is an extemporaneous situation that needs altering to your normal rules or laws. May I please be excused this time to attend to this emergency?" Her body language was already saying it via the tears. Had she not given the impression that the bully's power had been threatened he would have acquiesced to her request, feeling as though he still had control of the environment and his laws had not been violated.

Even in emergency situations you can think of some what-if scenarios that would occur if a certain thing happened and how you would respond. Knowing his demeanor and knowing that one day anyone in the class might have any type of situation that causes them to break his laws, you can think, "If this happened to me how would I react?" That's another reason I say, "You're always negotiating." The more you contemplate future situations that might impact your life, the better you can formulate plans to address them. Then, when they occur you'll have plans ready to address them.

In another situation, a female college professor offered a male student an opportunity to earn a better grade by sleeping with her. If the male student did not want such advances he could have rebuked her offer and told higher authorities. But being a male, he took advantage of the offer, and got the higher grade and the extra benefits that went along with them. Sometimes a bullying situation can appear to be advantageous in the moment, but you should also consider what the situation might look like in the future (that is, what's acceptable today may come back to bite you tomorrow).

Exoplanetary astronomer Sarah Ballard went public about the sexual advances of her mentor, Geoff Marcy of the University of California at Berkley. In describing the impact on her, Ballard said she harbored feelings of guilt and fear and the knowledge that she had no power. She wondered whether he'd only been saying she showed promise (as a student) to get closer to her. An investigation uncovered numerous charges of sexual harassment against Marcy and led to his resignation and a public apology.[1]

The point is you must be mindful of what you're going to do in any situation that might occur, especially when you know who it is that you're dealing with. Later in this chapter I will discuss the psychological and emotional costs of bullying.

FINANCIAL COSTS OF WORKPLACE BULLYING

Some of the costs of bullying in a work environment can be tied to dollars and cents. There is turnover from people who are exposed to bullying behavior. Perhaps they complained to a person who they think is a powerful figure within the environment and nothing changed. The bully's behavior wears down the individuals to the point that they don't want to come to work. They're not engaged. They feel defeated. There's increased absenteeism. We know from a company's standpoint that every time an employee leaves a facility and a new person is hired there's a training period that has a cost associated with it.

Dr. Renee Thompson specializes in consulting with healthcare facilities about bullying. She says:

> If we were to look at actual dollars, one of the statistics I use quite often is when we look at how bullying impacts retention and profits. We know workplace bullying has been linked to intent to leave and poor productivity. The estimated replacement costs are anywhere from $30,000 to $100,000 per year per individual. If we are talking about a specialty nurse, it's upward toward $145,000 per year.
>
> There was a statistic that came out a couple of years ago that studies showed that out of all the new nurses who quit their first job within the first six months 60 percent of them were quitting because of the bad behavior of their coworkers.[2]

As one example, a surgeon who bullies the staff in the operating room (OR) creates a cost. The individuals in the OR are in a closed environment. There's no way to walk away from bad behavior in an operating room. That surgeon who behaves as a bully ends up costing the facility money in the form of turnover, absenteeism, and low morale. The hospital has traditionally looked at the surgeon as a person who brings a lot of patients and revenue into the hospital. In the past, hospital administrations did not necessarily look at the cost associated with bullying behavior.

In the 2008, the Joint Commission, which accredits a lot of hospitals, used a sentinel event alert that focused on disruptive behavior.[3] Even though it was issued to discourage disruptive behavior, there are a lot of healthcare facilities still to this day that don't know how to effectively manage bullying behavior and are afraid of the loss of revenue by removing a physician from the staff who is behaving in that way.

There is also a human cost from bullying in health care. Dr. Thompson shares this example with nurses:

> It's 2:00 in the morning. You're concerned about your patient and you think you need to call the physician. When you look on the on-call schedule you see it's a physician notorious for screaming at nurses and making them feel like they're stupid. You say, "I'm not calling him, he's nasty." A new nurse overhears this and when that new nurse is in the same situation six months from now that new nurse makes the same decision.
>
> There's a different way of handling and addressing workplace bullying when it comes to health care because of the patient factor. When we find that organization that has a high incidence of bullying, it has the worst patient outcomes for numerous reasons.

Get access to the full interview with Dr. Renee Thompson at *http://themasternegotiator.com/negotiating-with-a-bully*.

There is a cost associated with negative outcomes happening to patients. Dr. Alan Rosenstein defines these as "adverse events."[4]

> Adverse events are dreadful things that happen that really should not happen. Now, terrible things should never happen at all. They typically occur 1 to two percent of the time. Our surveys

have shown that these adverse events can occur as much as 15 to 20 percent of the time related to disruptive behavior. A lot of these adverse events can be potentially prevented by improving communication. In fact, the Joint Commission has said that 70 percent of these adverse events can be traced back to problems with communication.

Not all those problems can be traced or linked directly to disruptive behavior, but a lot of them can. So, there is the cost of those adverse events, the cost of recruitment and retention, and the costs in liability.

When negotiating in any work environment, one form of leverage is the cost a bullying behavior has in an environment because most leaders are directly responsible for their organization's bottom line. When you talk about the cost of disruptive behavior, such insight will usually capture their attention.

Dana Davis, a university professor, full-time doctoral student, and the founder of the Asheville Nurses Support Group, recalls a bullying environment that drove her out of a nursing position. She was hired by a company that ran more than 40 primary care practices. There were a lot of safety concerns, such as unlicensed personnel running these practices without the requisite knowledge. Shortly after Dana started she went to a staff meeting at which one of the unlicensed personnel had terrible body language, such as slouching in her seat, yawning so others could see and hear her, and rolling her eyes in disagreement. Dana recalls:

> When I acknowledged it in the meeting, she immediately be-came belligerent, not so much with me but with her peers. I ended up having to send her home immediately. I thought that she was going to become physically aggressive. I thought if I don't, this was my moment, and this was going to set the tone for my experience here because I was the clinical manager of these three practices.
>
> I came to find out that this was what had been going on the year before I got there. All these medical assistants and un-licensed personnel had just been bullying each other and the

providers. They had all just been at each other's throats for the entire year and this is what I had been told after this meeting when I sent this lady home. The physician providers were intimidated by the staff. It was just really a crazy culture.

I took some privileges away from some of the unlicensed personnel who were making medication errors. I would not allow them to give vaccines until they had completed reading "To Err is Human" by the Institute of Medicine. I received pushback from their physician providers who said, "No, they can give vaccines." I insisted, "No, they can't because they're incompetent until we get these things rectified."

Within a month or two the leadership team and the nurse administration were freezing me out of meetings and not returning emails. There was a lot of talk behind my back that they weren't happy with me. I would go to them and do what most normal people would do and say, "What have I done? What do I need to do differently?" They said, "Oh no you're doing fine." "That's not what I'm hearing. I'm getting the cold shoulder and people who had been super friendly to me in the past suddenly wouldn't work with me."

I can't even begin to tell you how nasty they were to each other. There was a person under me who was a medical assistant and she had been a medical assistant for twenty-plus years; she was a delightful person. She cried every other day. I don't know if they called her names, but they would slam doors in her face. They refused to do the work that was assigned by her. They claimed that she was racist, and it wasn't the case at all.

It was a very toxic environment, one I had never experienced before, and I've been in health care for twenty-three years. One of the physicians to this day tells me that she is still suffering some of the effects of the environment and this was almost two years ago. We had at least four or five physician providers leave during that year. To me that's almost unheard of. It was just the most toxic environment I have ever worked in. I had seen where physician providers had been super demanding, but the unlicensed personnel were the ones who were treating everybody badly. I left that job after a year and have since learned that other nurses hired into the position left after a brief time.

At that job I was making probably close to $80,000 and I left to make $3,600 a semester teaching at a college. I left for pennies and was totally fine to do that. I didn't even know how I was going to live, but I couldn't stay another day. It was mainly an emotionally taxing situation. I sought counseling.

Dana considered but did not pursue a whistleblower's lawsuit. One attorney candidly told her that if she filed a claim she would never get a job again in that city. Get access to the full interview with Dana Davis at *http://themasternegotiator.com/negotiating-with-a-bully.*

Regardless of the work-place environment you find yourself in, when management is intimidated by the staff, that speaks to the strength of the staff and lack of strength of management. That's also a situation that you'll rarely find, which makes it all the more unique. If you ever find yourself in such an environment be cautious. The normal things you'd do, such as go to management to inform them of a negative situation, might just get you fired. If you were confronting an egregious situation, you might consider forming a coalition consisting of the strongest management supporter you could attract, along with representatives from staff who are aligned with your views.

In looking at some of the costs associated with bullying I've mentioned turnover, low morale, and absenteeism. There are also financial settlements with victims. Another cost is the cost of litigation for medical malpractice suits and employment suits. In cases where physicians have lost their privileges from the hospital because of acting disruptively, they are suing to get back on staff. There are litigation costs involved with disruptive behavior, discipline, and sanctions.

With all the financial costs for an employer, why does bullying behavior continue? One of the things that you always must consider is: What is so important to this entity that it allows certain behavior to occur? Consider the case of the administration staff who ignores the behavior of a bully physician because the doctor is bringing in a lot of business to the hospital. The way to combat that doctor and to show the hospital staff this behavior should stop is to paint a picture of what might possibly happen if this doctor's behavior became public knowledge. People would start associating the doctor's behavior with the hospital, which would lead to a mass exodus of patients and staff from that hospital. The reputation of the hospital would be so tarnished that people wouldn't even want to be treated by a doctor associated with that hospital and thus other doctors would disassociate themselves with that hospital.

Dr. Alan Rosenstein confirms, "If the hospital is not on top of bullying, they get into the newspapers. They get on TV. The staff does not want to go there, the patients do not want to go there, and they cannot recruit new doctors or new nurses."[5]

The negotiation strategy is to tie in as many negative consequences that might occur in the future as possible that would result from the doctor's behavior going unchecked and to encourage the hospital staff to stop the doctor's behavior. If you really want to talk about pinpointing cost and how one might combat an issue based on cost, you could always use leverage. Leverage aides your efforts when negotiating with a bully in any environment. You can also amass a force.

Let's say you surreptitiously went to the media as a whistleblower and said, "These are the behaviors that are going on in this hospital and the hospital is allowing it to occur." Now suddenly, the hospital is getting unwanted attention, which might affect their bottom line and they don't want that to happen. Now they're going to address the doctor's behavior. You must highlight the loss of revenue to cause the other person, the bully, to alter his perception and actions.

If you marshal powerful forces and the entity still doesn't back down from those larger forces, be prepared to have even greater forces on standby to thwart the bully's efforts. Strike at the bully's power source in waves of attacks. With each wave, you want to make the wave stronger than the previous one.

You can imply that something bigger is coming if you don't acquiesce to this, but be ready to stand up to the bully by having your next piece of negotiation strategy ready. Address the financial costs to the entity that is substantiating the bully's actions.

The costs of bullying may encompass financial as well as psychological and emotional costs. Take, for example, a well-publicized incident that took place in a Utah hospital emergency department. A nurse was arrested by a police officer because she refused to withdraw a blood sample from an unconscious patient. The nurse conferred with her superior and told the officer about the hospital's policy about drawing blood. She told the officer that she was talking to her supervisor on the phone and he was the one citing policy. The officer insisted on overriding the rules. His body camera captured footage of him handcuffing the nurse and pulling her out of the emergency department. The municipality eventually paid a settlement of $500,000 because of the officer's actions.[6]

Consider what type of circumstances you might be confronted with and how you might respond. The officer did not handle the situation well when the nurse stated she was following hospital policy in refusing to take blood.

One possible way to combat a situation when both parties consider themselves to be following policy is to appeal to a higher authority. In the case of the nurse she could have handed the phone to the officer to let him speak directly with her supervisor. By doing that, she would have taken herself out of the line of fire and the situation would have been dealt with by the officer and her supervisor. The latter was not in the same environment, which would have left the officer with no one to handcuff, unless he still wanted to go after the nurse.

Who really does pays the settlement? The town residents might face an increase in taxes. The police force will now have a different mindset about how they're going to go about handling incidents in their municipality. There is a cost associated with well-publicized incidents. Today one person's behavior as a bully is broadcast to millions of people. In the case of the police officer in the Utah emergency department, the video was released by the nurse who had access to the footage from the body camera. Other nurses, healthcare providers, and the public saw that video. The impact was magnified all over the country with emergency nurses concerned about their own safety with police officers, leading to questioning about the appropriate way to handle such a situation. The security guards who did not intervene and protect her from the police came under attack as did the police officer who was fired.

You can imagine the pressure that was placed on the police chief, the city council, the mayor, and so on. None of them wanted that stigma. You can point to that example and relate it to a bullying situation. Tell the bully, "You do not want this to happen to you, do you?" See if the bullying entity changes his or her behavior.

When there's too great a cost to pay in any environment, that environment will change. Finding that price point is what you need to do when negotiating against a bully so that you thwart the bully's efforts.

David Dadian, owner of *www.powersolution.com*, describes how the actions of a COO ultimately resulted in the COO losing his own high-paying job.

> My first impression of a client's new COO was that he was trouble. I said, "He's going to live by the sword and die by the sword. This guy is dangerous. He is going to die by the sword." The COO became brash. Finally, it came down to him asking us our opinion on a project and solution. We said, "Don't advise it. Here's why."

> The COO ignored the advice and moved ahead with the plan to implement the solution. "The whole project began, and we told the COO, 'We're hands off. This is your baby. This is your project. We're not involved in it. Take full responsibility and full accountability. It's yours.' As predicted, the implementation was rife with problems. My company provided support to assist the client on an emergency basis.

> When this COO made these changes, they lost two solid weeks of production. At that point they had close to seventy employees who could do very little for two weeks. They had clients

who were not happy. They couldn't deliver their projects to their clients because this gentleman decided to pick everything up and move it into an untested territory. They had problem after problem.

We sent our bill (for the intense support needed to remedy the problem) and I got a phone call from the COO. He said, "I can't believe you have the audacity to bill us this amount of money," I said, "Excuse me! You had my guys working around the clock for three days. I had three engineers around the clock. I am more than fair. I could bill you $20,000, but I billed you $6,000. I believe that's more than fair."

"You're going to have to do something with this and if you don't change your attitude you're not going to keep this account," said the COO.

With that I just hung up the phone. I went to my service manager and my VP of sales. I said, "Please prepare a Termination of Services notification for the company" and they just looked at me. I said, "Send it out immediately," which they did. I said, "If you're going to threaten me, you have threatened the wrong guy." I sent a Termination of Services to the client, saying, "You've got thirty days. We're removing our services and you're on your own."

That just began the whole spiral. I was on the phone with the CEO. I was on the phone with the consultant. They were begging us to stay. I said, "It's really simple. Either he goes, or we go. If you're not letting him go, we're gone." We were gone and within three months he was gone.

He was certainly a bully. He certainly made a threat and he wasn't capable of following through on his threats. I don't allow anyone to threaten me personally, certainly not my people and not my organization. We just terminated them and that shocked my director of business development that we would walk away from an account like that. I said, "It's not about the money. It's about being respected for what you do."

Get access to the full interview with David Dadian at *http://the-masternegotiator.com/negotiating-with-a-bully*

In another situation, a pharmaceutical sales representative stood up to a bully. Yolonda Royster explains:

> I was providing food for a physician's office, so I could speak with the doctor and the staff about my product. In doing so I brought enough food for everyone, however there was a budget that I needed to adhere to. When I arrived, I was told by the office manager, who also happened to be the doctor's wife, that the budget that I provided them with was not what they were accustomed to. If I wanted to continue coming there to speak with them and bring lunch I would need to increase my budget. I said to her, "It looks like there was enough food left over for everyone. Is there a problem?" She said, "This is not what we expect, and we don't want you to come back here if you can't do what we want you to do."

> In that scenario I felt like I was being bullied. She was trying to get more out of me than what I was able to offer based on the rules of my company. I explained that this was what my budget is; this is what I would be able to provide and if it's not enough then I would not be coming back.

> That's what I did. I do have a budget that I could play with and that is what I also chose. Part of it is my company's regulations, but I also manage my budget. For that physician's office, that was what I wanted to do. Because of the way that I perceived their attitudes and their lack of respect for what I was doing, I decided not to go back. As a result, they have missed out on some of the opportunities to have conversations with me over lunch in the future.

Get access to the full interview with Yolonda Royster at *http://the-masternegotiator.com/negotiating-with-a-bully*.

EMOTIONAL AND PSYCHOLOGICAL COSTS

Bullying can cause deep, lasting scars and stunted emotional growth. Targets of bullies discuss the loss of trust they develop. Earlier in this chapter I referred to Brady Paterson, who was bullied at home by his stepfather. He was also bullied at school.

That caused me to have less of an ability to relate to people. I would just retreat. My life moved into books. I spent all my time reading, hiding from people, and playing video games. I was watching TV and doing anything that I could do to escape my day-to-day life because it wasn't very pleasant. I was very reclusive most of my life. If I wasn't hiding in a tree, I was reading or hiding in a bush playing by myself. I didn't play a lot with other kids because I just very quickly learned that it wasn't safe to be with other people. I had to protect myself by being elsewhere, which meant I didn't have to get violent to protect myself.

I always had to be on the lookout for who's going to hurt me next. That's a thing I've taken into not just my business relationships in the past, but my intimate relationships as well where I'm always wondering what's going to happen next. It's left me a little gun-shy. I think it's the big reason why I ended up teaching survival skills. It's because that's how I felt most of my life.

Even though I kind of drifted through distinct groups I primarily hung out with one crowd. It was another way to protect myself. I knew that if there was a fight my friends were the ones who would jump in and be happy to get involved whereas other groups of people who I spent time with would try to avoid fighting. My rougher crowd allowed me a certain amount of protection because I knew that if I was around these folks fights weren't a problem because they would have my back. ·

With that crowd came drug use and alcohol abuse. I developed a drug addiction until I was 21 and then I realized something had to change.

Today Brady is married and runs a survival training company.

Caitlin Binnie, the young girl we read about earlier in the chapter, is also scarred. Her mother says:

> She has such a fear of being out in social circumstances, being picked on and being called out as the tattletale or the one who was the bully. One of the biggest reasons she is homeschooled is she fears being picked on again. It has affected the last four years of her life. Any time she's entrusted herself with a friend or somebody with bowling or somebody in any of the extracurricular activities, that girl always tends to turn on her. She always says, "Mom, I guess I'm doing something wrong and it's all because of me." With different psychologists, we've slowly gotten her to have some self-confidence and some self-esteem. She still has an issue of ever trusting people because she's afraid that the minute she trusts someone she's going to get picked on and bullied again.
>
> I think the words that are used just stay with us longer. Those words are never going to go away. It's a matter of dealing with that word. If you're called a loser, if you're called a bitch, or if you're called a mama's girl, those words are always going to be out in the community and unless you let go of the terror that came with the words, the words will always be there to haunt you.
>
> I think Caitlin will shy away from even going to a university. She is working right now and has developed some friendships at her work because it's a completely different world. Although it's just a part-time job, she tends to cling to that more so than anything she's ever done in life. I have a feeling as a result she may just decide to do a few courses here and there. I don't know if she will excel and move forward in any post-secondary education because of the fear of being ridiculed.
>
> It's a sad situation, but her mental stability is more important for her than any degree or any further education that she might get in a school format. I think it's just going to bring her back to

how bad it was in junior high and high school. She's going to be faced with that fear of it all happening again. It's very hard for her to trust people because she was so trusting and so willing to give people a chance, a second chance, and a third chance, and it just exploded every time.

Caitlin's experience is indicative of the way some females bully others. Rather than resorting to fighting, many female bullies use subtle forms of aggression. They are often socially adept and use manipulation, the silent treatment, ostracism, and other hurtful behavior to bully others. They may be abusive to friends and may act as ringleaders in subtly undermining their friends' self-esteem. The female bully may act in authoritarian ways to threaten others with withdrawing friendship when the bully's authority is questioned.[7]

Dr. Renee Thompson describes the impact on nurses of being bullied:

I've talked to so many nurses who have said they feel physically ill on their way to work, especially if they know that they're going to be working with some of the people who are behaving in ways that would be considered bullying.

This is taking the joy out of why they became a nurse to begin with. People go into this profession because they want to help. They want to make a difference in the lives of other people, but when you're faced with day after day of dealing with coworkers who you can't trust and who treat you in an unprofessional manner and target you, you start to question the decision that you made to become a nurse in the first place.

There is a lot of the psychological stress. A lot of nurses suffer from post-traumatic stress disorder because of a bullying situation and some of them can no longer work because they can't get past the psychological damage of dealing with that type of behavior day in and day out.

I'll share one example. I was doing a short workshop that was two-and-a-half hours. There was a nurse in my audience who was really quiet the whole time. She never showed any emotion and I started getting a little concerned about her. I thought this might be somebody who doesn't want to be here, doesn't think she needs to be here, or is really struggling with something and is going to stay back. She's going to stay after while everybody leaves and sure enough she stayed after.

It took her ten minutes to compose herself because she was crying. She shared with me that she had dealt with somebody who bullied her as a new nurse and this went on for about a year. It got so bad to the point where she had to transfer to another unit. She said that every day she's so petrified that she's going to run into her that she never goes to the coffee shop. She always packs her lunch because she's so afraid that she might run into her.

I said to her, "How long ago did this happen?" It was five years ago, and she was still traumatized by this one nurse. Of course, I recommended that she gets some professional help. She still was traumatized by this. I can give you numerous other examples of nurses who truly suffer from some level of post-traumatic stress disorder to the point where they're no longer able to work.

As a teacher, Dona Ramsey encountered supervisors who were bullies. Each supervisor suffered a cost associated with bullying behavior. The experiences left Dona feeling demeaned, humiliated, and like she was a first-grader. In her first job, after she checked her mailbox her administrator would put a written message in it.

She would reprimand me for not following through on the note that she had placed in my mailbox. This happened on several occasions. She would also come up behind me and very softly say things with horrible language, and threaten me if I didn't do what she wanted or how she wanted it done. She put roadblocks up when I tried to present music programs with the children. I came into teaching when I was in my 40s. Her behavior made me angry and more determined to be successful.

That year I kept a journal in a spiral notebook on both sides of the pages dated and timed in ink, and that actually was used in the meeting where the teachers' union was severely reprimanding her. I was able to state dates and times of incidents that had happened. She was placed within the district administration and eventually left the district.

My second supervisor belittled me and told me to get a timer so that I could be precisely punctual to within two or three seconds of starting and ending class with my elementary students. I was told this in front of another teacher and treated like I was a second-grade student, so I bought a timer and set it. I figured that would keep her happy. She assigned me a small room where there was no room for movement or instruments. It was literally a closet that was used later by a kindergarten teacher for a storage room. It was underneath the gymnasium, so when balls were bouncing you could not be heard. I felt this was a deliberate act on her part. The supervisor became mentally ill during the school year and resigned.

In a third situation, my principal closed the door and told me I *would* be happy to be the pianist for a school play production that took up about three months of time. I would do that, and if I ever told anyone that I had been threatened I would be called a liar by my boss. That boss also told me, "Any idiot can come in off the street and teach music or physical education."

That principal later got very frustrated with a student; he struck the child in the head with a teacher's textbook. He ended up in court and he will never be allowed again to work with children.

I had another experience with a supervisor who was very intimidated by me because at that point I had a state association position that gave me a lot of credibility. I was a female and he wasn't happy that a female had that much power. He leered at me a couple of times in his office with the door shut and made threats to me that I would do this or I wouldn't do that. I went ahead and did what needed to be done because it was best for children.

Ultimately his name was submitted for a state association president position and I was on the nominating committee. Although I didn't say anything directly, the chairman of the nominating committee picked up on my body language and asked me what the problem was. I simply stated that person didn't have very good people skills. My reaction blocked his hopes for the state president.

In another situation, I encountered a bully working as a volunteer for a state-level organization. I simply withdrew from the role and decided I didn't need to put up with the behavior. I left that person in a bit of bind because that person needed my help, but I was done. I just simply walked away and feel to this day that I did the right thing. That person continues to reach out to me and I want nothing to do with them. I'm done. I don't need to put up with that anymore.

There are two times in a teacher's career of particular vulnerability: your first three years you're not tenured. They don't have to renew your contract for any reason whatsoever, so it's common knowledge that the first three years you put up with whatever comes your way. If you can't put up with it, you're probably not going to be renewed and you're going to need to find a different career. You're very vulnerable. You must suck it up and deal with it, and deal with it the best way you can and not let it destroy you.

You are also vulnerable when you are very close to retirement. I spent eight years teaching staff development to other teachers on a national level. The school district punished me for that and docked my pay, which ultimately affected my retirement. There was nothing that I could do about it. They would not allow me to use accumulated sick time or vacation time to cover those days off. They realized it was a way to cut their costs. During the last five years of teaching I probably lost between $45,000 and $50,000 income. That ultimately affected my rate of retirement pay.

Get access to the full interview with Dona Ramsey at *http://the-masternegotiator.com/negotiating-with-a-bully.*

Chuck Sutherland recalls how he felt when he was bullied. "I felt humiliation, rage, and worthlessness. I would come home from school, go to my room, and cry when they would throw my stuff out the window."

Chuck is now involved in real estate, where he also encounters bullies. The experiences stimulate all those thoughts and feelings about what he went through as a kid.

> The history never goes away. It's always right there being linked up in the brain. It's interesting because my strategies still haven't changed to deal with those people, but now I don't have any interest in their approval or business. I'm just not going to do business with people who are like that. They, in fact, lose. It ends up being their loss because for the most part (maybe except for the Northeast part of the country, big-dollar real-estate deals, and Las Vegas are exceptions), the bullies end up losing more than they gain. They lose zoning cases, for example, in the real estate business. They don't get financing. Who wants to make a loan to somebody who is going to be a jerk?

> Some people will not follow this advice, to their chagrin. If I am raising money for a real estate deal, I look at their partners. If they have somebody who is overbearing, demanding, and nasty, I just don't put them in the deal. If I'm doing development consulting for somebody today and they're acting again with that same overbearing manner, I just don't have to deal with them.

> From what I've seen, particularly in business, is the bully who bullies on purpose is just nasty. Or I see the bully who speaks all

nice and sweet to you and at the end of the night they're putting a knife in your gut. They don't rise in the estimation of their peers, at least in the circles that I run in. In the part of the country I live in, if business is built on relationships, then how are you going to build good relationships if you treat people like crap?

The outcome of bullying is not always negative. Dubbed YouTube's "style queen," Bethany Mota built an empire because of being bullied. As a lonely 13-year-old, she found solace in making videos devoted to beauty, style, and do-it-yourself projects. Bethany's YouTube channel has nearly a billion views, and she launched a fashion line with Aeropostale, has been on *Dancing with the Stars*, and released a pop single.[8]

Sarah Hyland (*Modern Family* star and creative director for Candie's) has been the target of online bullying. She has had a lifelong struggle with kidney dysplasia, which caused her weight to fluctuate. She was a target of people who mocked her for being too thin or too fat. She said, "It is important, no matter where you are in life, to be proud of yourself. Do not let people's hateful words get to you. Surround yourself with people who make you feel good."[9]

REDUCING THE COSTS OF BULLIES

In a work setting, an employer has leverage to stop bullying. The manager can say you're fired or you will be fired if you don't alter your behavior. Suppose the bully responds by using his leverage: "I really have the power here; you don't. I'm the owner's nephew." In this case the nephew, even though he is a subordinate, is bullying the manager.

The manager tells the owner, "Your nephew is bullying other individuals. If this continues, we will lose productivity as the result of absenteeism. We will lose potential business opportunities simply because of the emotional toll that his antics are taking on others in the department. I am bringing this to your attention, so you will address it."

In that case the manager is taking more control but also running a risk of the owner saying, "I don't care. He's my sister's kid and whatever he says is right. Stay out of his way or else you go."

There are some cases in which you need to get out of an environment because the mental or physical cost of staying there can be too great. You must make that decision based on the attempts you have made to alter the situation and the cooperation you have had with others, especially superiors, to assist in altering the behavior that you're trying to address. If you can't get it, you need to get out of the environment in which bullying behavior exists.

Brady Paterson's abuse stopped when he was forced out of his home. "I got kicked out at 17 years old because I had defended my mom at the dinner table and my stepfather said, 'You're going to leave my house now and do not come back.' My mom went along with it. I moved out. My stepfather was abusing my siblings. They didn't tell me until many years later. Because of the crowd that I hung out with and my lifestyle, they were worried that I would go to jail for killing him, so they didn't want to tell me that he was abusing them as well. My mother left him four years after I left."

There is a lot of reluctance to face the unpleasant reality of bullying. Suppose you're a subordinate and you want to fight back. You talk to your manager, who says, "I can't believe that's happening. You must be imagining it. You know we really need that person in the company. He's very valuable. Can you just ignore it? We don't like trouble-makers here. Everybody has to pull together for the sake of the company and if you continue to raise this issue you're going to find yourself blocked in terms of raises or advancements, so just be quiet."

That happened with a TV network where one of their star anchors paid thirty-two million dollars as hush money right before he was fired.[10]

The bullying boss eventually pays a price too. Suppose the boss tells her staff, "You can't have your vacation time because we need you here at the office." She does that to one person after another and then suddenly the boss is in a position where she must have the staff work overtime. They collectively say, "Not today. Not this time. This is when we choose to fight." The timing of it should have the maximum effect when the boss is really in the direst of situations. That's when you take that power away. The staff says, "We're not going to. You have to fend for yourself."

If the staff says, "We'll do it for you this time" the risk is that the bully will think, "I got away with it this time and I can get away with it again." You need to understand the bully's mindset and either hold that bully's feet to the fire by not giving in or, if you do acquiesce, understand where you may be leading yourself.

Individuals who have not been content to allow the costs of bullying to mount have used the power of social media or others to get attention. This uses another form of leverage to bring attention to what's happening. There may be a price to pay for being a whistleblower. What occurred in the movie industry with Harvey Weinstein was his threat of blacklisting women who were not cooperative with his sexual demands. He was a bully and some women acquiesced to those demands, but there were some who went to the police, gained leverage, and started wiretapping him in conversations. There are ways to combat a bully if you choose to do so and you are willing to incur the price. That determination is yours.

In Harvey Weinstein's case, his behavior continued for decades as people reported incidents that occurred in the 1990s, the 2000s, and as late as 2010. People knew about it in the industry and no one chose to do anything about it. The timing wasn't right to exact the cost.

In Conclusion

Keep cost in mind when you confront bullying. Present it to those whose actions you want to alter by highlighting the cost they will have to bear if you should choose to bring others into the environment. That is a threat. "If you do this, here's what I'm going to do." You need to know at what point in time you should address a bully's actions depending on the environment you're in. Be mindful of the setting and how it affects what you do to show you're not a person to be messed with.

I've highlighted the economic loss, the psychological costs, and the atmosphere that can be established when a bully's behavior is unchecked. We've discussed that people who are being bullied may be unaware of any attempts to control the bully's behavior and the feeling of being defeated, of not being supported, and of having to hide to avoid the individual.

When someone is bullying you, you must let them know that you are not going to take it to the degree that you possibly could. If you don't, the cost of not doing so will just increase until you do eventually address it. Just be mindful of what is going on in any environment and to what degree you need to regain control of the situation.

HOMEWORK

Find a person who has been bullied. Ask about the effects that person experienced.

6

Putting It All Together

Kendra watched the neurosurgeon walk up the hall to where she stood outside the nurse's station. She could tell from his expression that he was fuming. In a loud voice he demanded, "Why are the vital signs from this morning not entered into the computer? How can I tell what is going on with my patients unless you nurses do your jobs?" As he advanced on her, Kendra observed two visitors and a patient standing in the hall watching the scene.

"Dr. Rizzo, come with me into the conference room where we can discuss your concerns."

"I am *not* moving until you give me an explanation."

"Dr. Rizzo, you are angry about the vital signs. Your tone is upsetting this patient and his parents. I would like to resolve this issue with you in the conference room. Come with me now." Without looking over her shoulder, Kendra entered the conference room. She heard the door close behind her after Dr. Rizzo joined her.

WHO IS AROUND THE BULLY?

Use the environment as an ally when you're confronting a bully. Consider the story of Kendra and Dr. Rizzo. Kendra told the doctor that they should go into a different environment in which they could converse in a more civil manner, away from the patients who were observing the scene he was creating. In that situation, Kendra could have been inviting more conflict if Dr. Rizzo had denied her request or chosen not to follow her.

Note that Kendra said they should go into the room where they could speak privately, turned her back to him, and walked through the door while communicating through her body language, "Follow me." She removed him from an environment in which he had more power (or thought he had more power) and in which he perceived himself as being in control. He also had an audience there. That location was altered simply because Kendra changed the environment and took that extra sense of importance away from him through the people who he may have been showing off for.

In another example, the editor of *Vanity Fair*, Graydon Carter, recounted an incident that took place in a restaurant. As he walked past movie producer Harvey Weinstein, who sat at a table with young starlets, Harvey called Graydon over to complain about some perceived slight and said he was going to come at Graydon with *Talk* magazine, which he was about to launch. As the two men began to argue, Harvey said, "Let's settle this outside." Graydon expected they would get into a fist fight.

When they got outside, Harvey did not hit him. Instead, he turned on "one of his famous charm offensives" and complimented Graydon about *Vanity Fair* and said he hoped *Talk* would be half as good. When Harvey tried to pat Graydon on the shoulder, Graydon took a step back and got in his car. "It was only on the way home that I realized the challenge had been a show intended to impress the table full of attractive young women."[1]

That's why you need to be especially aware of the environment when you engage with any type of individual with whom you're negotiating and even more so with a bully. The environment can serve as his ally— or it can be yours—depending on exactly what you do in that setting. Change the environment to take its power away from the bully. You can do so by changing the venue by stating, "Let's talk another time," thereby getting yourself out of that environment and seeing if he will follow you.

In the case of Kendra and Dr. Rizzo, the fact that Dr. Rizzo followed her indicated that she had the power in that exchange. She was also able to reclaim her power by moving the neurosurgeon away from his seat of power and to where the patients could not hear what was being said. She could have become more aggressive with him if she chosen to do so.

The environment you choose to negotiate in is also important because the person who is in control of the environment has an advantage in the negotiations.

You may be familiar with something in the healthcare environment called a "Code Blue" when a patient is having a serious cardiac episode. Because the healthcare environment is currently very concerned about bullying, the concept of calling a "Code Pink" has been proposed. This means when a bully starts going after a nurse, anyone who is on the nursing unit comes away from what they are doing, stands in a circle together, and stares at the person who is ranting. It has the effect of stopping the behavior because of the audience observing the behavior. The power shifts to the nurse because of the alteration in the environment.

The power shift affects the dynamics of the interaction. The bully thinks, "I'm talking to you as a one-on-one and I'm going to bully you as a one-on-one. Now there are others who are observing; they look like they are on your side. They have your back, which means there's more power against me now. I better retreat. I am being over powered."

The Code Pink response could possibly backfire depending on the type of bully one is dealing with. Referring to the situation described in Chapter 5 of a Utah nurse who was handcuffed for refusing to draw blood, this nurse did have a support system in the form of her supervisor, who tried to reason with the police officer. The security guards in the environment did not intervene when the police officer lost control.

If more individuals had stood up to the officer and told him, "You shouldn't be doing that" the outcome might have been different. If the staff stared at him, surrounded him, and talked to him to get him to calm down, he may have been able to back down from his increasingly unreasonable actions. He did not, and he still felt as though he was the one with the authority. The incident occurred in a busy emergency department after a lengthy discussion, so the nursing staff did not have the ability to divert their attention away from patients to get involved in the disagreement.

Considering the suggestions just mentioned, if any of these had been implemented, the officer might have called for backup, which also would have escalated the situation. It bears repeating: Before engaging in an action consider the consequences of those actions related to you losing more control of the situation. In a Code Pink action in which other nurses surround their beleaguered colleague the doctor could become more belligerent and think to himself, "Okay so now it's eight of you against me. That's even. Let me just show you how tough I can really be now." You must be careful of the tactics you employ based on the mindset of an individual with whom you are negotiating, especially when it comes to a bully. You should know what will make him back down and what won't. Be prepared with alternative strategies if he doesn't retreat.

KNOWING THE BULLY

Before confronting a bully, you need to truly understand his characteristics and mannerisms. This allows you to anticipate the tactics he might plan to use as well as to identify the strategies he is carrying out. By doing so you can determine what strategies to use to further your goals.

In some cases, you may not know if the person you are interacting with is a bully because the first encounter you have reveals the nature of the bully. Nevertheless, you can position him so that you address his objectives ahead of time. Accomplish this by talking about the process you will be going through during the negotiation. Discuss the phases of the negation and how you foresee the nature of the interactions you're going to have. If he objects to the fact that something wasn't the way he thought it was going to be, you can refer to the conversation you had about how the negotiation was going to transpire.

Adjust your strategy depending on the insights you gather as you engage with him from one point to the next. The bully will typically give clues to his intent to escalate the negotiation and become a little more aggressive.

WRITTEN AGREEMENTS

Before the bully becomes aggressive and unreasonable, it is ideal to document your understanding of what you have both agreed to. Get it in writing so you have something that shows your areas of agreement. If you think you're going to be in a situation with someone who will become overly aggressive, turn into a bully, or start to use bullying tactics, you might even want his signature on the agreement. This written agreement forms the basis for locking in the bully to an understanding and strengthens your position should he not fulfill the terms of the agreement. However, a written agreement does not always stop a bully, as the following story illustrates.

A good-hearted man became friendly with a homeless couple and decided to let them stay with him in his one-bedroom apartment. In June, the couple signed an agreement stating how much rent they would pay the man. The first month the couple paid less than the agreed-upon amount. The second month and every month thereafter, they paid nothing. They began complaining the man woke them up when he used the kitchen in the morning next to the living room where they were sleeping. After five months of not receiving any additional rent from the couple and several conversations about the lack of rent, the man asked them to leave. They informed him it was now their apartment and they had no intention of leaving.

The man gave the husband an ultimatum (the wife was unaware of the plan) and a deadline of leaving by a certain Saturday in November. The man changed the lock on the apartment and with the help of friends moved their possessions out of the apartment onto a landing by the door. That night the couple broke into the apartment and moved back in. The man initiated a court proceeding to have them evicted, which was unsuccessful because he was not the landlord and had no legal authority to get them evicted. Ultimately, the man left his apartment and moved in with his mother. The couple continued to occupy the apartment, living rent free for more than nine months, until the landlord evicted them. The man's generous impulse to help turned into him being a victim of bullies who knew how to take advantage of squatters' rights.

In this case, the man clearly lost the battle with the bullies. In other situations, the outcome of your negotiation and your effectiveness in countering a bully is less clear. Observe what your action does to him: what actions he commits after you have done something, said something, or shown him a different thought process to make him change his position, even if it's ever so slight. If he changes his position, you know that you had some effect on him as to how he's evaluating what you said or did.

David Dadian of PowerSolution.com shares a story that centered around a negotiation with a potential client disputing something in writing. His sales call took place in a nasty-looking warehouse. David and an associate were well dressed in business suits. Their prospect (we'll call him Tony) sat at a desk covered with a ton of garbage. It was like walking into a hoarder's house. Tony was a hard, crusty older man who didn't even get up when David and his associate shook his hand. There weren't even chairs for the two visitors to use. During their sales presentation Tony either feigned or showed some interest in what they presented.

Once David finished his pitch he asked Tony if he had any questions. David also gave him an agreement that included terms and conditions, which Tony flipped through as David was talking to him. Tony said, "Let me ask you a question. If I didn't like your services, I could fire you at any moment so I'm not sure what these terms and conditions are. You expect me to sign these?"

David responded, "It goes both ways. If you read through the terms and conditions in its entirety we also have the right to fire *you*, so what makes you think we wouldn't fire you?" That caught the prospect by surprise; he was not expecting that rebuttal. David raised his voice a little to be emphatic.

Within a minute or so after David spoke, Tony warmed up. Tony felt David met him at his level and wasn't there to take any of his guff. He developed respect for David for coming in more so as an equal versus coming in trying to get one over on him.

Tony seemed to be the kind of gentleman who was always weary of a sales guy or a sales pitch. David said to him, "Look, Tony, I built my company just like you built your company—from the ground up. I'm a business owner just like you. I'm not pitching you here. You asked me to explain what it is we do that would help your business and I did. Did I once ask you for anything?"

"No," Tony replied.

David asked, "So why would you even think to go through our terms and conditions and just pick out the termination clause and say you can fire us?"

"I've had a number of guys like you come in here," said Tony.

David responded, "Uh-uh. Don't put me in that category. Don't paint me with that same brush. You've had other people come in and try to pull one over on you. You apparently took the same approach and they weren't successful."

"You're right."

"I'm not trying to sell you anything. I came in, stated what I was looking to do based on what you asked, and I'm leaving it in your hands. The decision is yours. It's no sweat off my back. Our services may not be the right fit for you whether it's price points, performance, or something else."

David noticed a substantial change in Tony's demeanor. He was more open and smiled more. However, a year later, he had still not agreed to use David's services.

Get access to the full interview with David Dadian at *http://the-masternegotiator.com/negotiating-with-a-bully*.

RESPONDING TO AUTHORITY ON THE SPOT

Years ago, I was a new speaker in an organization. I was asked if I would help with back-of-the-room sales. I agreed because I'm the type of person who will pitch in to do anything. As speakers, we were also told that we had an additional discount we could use as an incentive that the salespeople who were also selling in the back of the room did not have.

I encountered an individual who incorrectly thought he was in control of the sales force while I was talking with some individuals about purchasing some course materials. I was in the process of offering that extra discount and this individual said to me, "You can't do that" while he was addressing someone else trying to sell them some of the course materials. I looked at him and said, "Excuse me?" He said, "You can't offer that type of discount." I looked at him and I said, "Why are you saying that?" He said, "No, we're not allowed to." I said, "Don't worry about it." Next, he turned from the prospective customer he was speaking to and faced me. He said, "That's not allowed."

The prospective customers stood there looking at each other and then looking at what was going on with the two of us. I turned to face him. I took a step toward him and said, "We will discuss this in a moment." I used a stern tone and the body language gesture of stepping closer to him. He said, "Okay." He then went back and started dealing with his customer.

I knew the way I spoke, along with my body language gestures, affected his perspective of what he had been saying. After we dealt with our prospects he and I left the sales area and I told him, "First of all, don't you ever again do something like that to me in front of anyone. You don't know who I am, and you don't know what authority I have, so what would make you think that you can tell me that I would not be able to do something, especially in front of the prospective customers?" He stuttered. "Well, I thought, I thought…"

When I perceived he was attempting to bully me, I put him back in his place as quickly as I did simply because I wanted to let him know to never do that again. He realized if he did it again there would be more severe consequences. I watched him after this exchange. He was subdued and submissive. That's a way you can tell to what degree your interaction has had some effectiveness with the other individual or bully.

Let's say the bully escalates his attacks after you said something that should have calmed him down. In the case of Kendra and Dr. Rizzo, suppose Kendra had reacted to Dr. Rizzo's rant by saying, "Doctor, you're right." That would have emboldened him to continue such behavior in the future, and forced her to realize that her tactics were ineffective in stopping his behavior. Watch the actions that occur after you initiate an action to determine to what degree they have been effective.

There are often alternatives to use to dampen the bully's effort to belittle you. For instance, you've gone through a series of rebuttals and you're not getting anywhere, and the bully is persisting. You can use leverage, such as the Code Pink maneuver. This is the use of leverage in the form of other individuals whose presence causes the bully to become subdued.

In hospitals, for example, the Joint Commission has a standard that there should be zero tolerance for disruptive behavior. The staff is educated on what that means and the consequences for violating the behavioral norms. For physicians, that may mean loss of privileges to care for patients at that hospital.

In the healthcare context, disruptive behavior has specific implications. It includes abusive language, condescending behavior, belittling individuals in front of their peers, calling them out publicly, and ranting and raving. It also includes non-compliance, that is, not making themselves available when they need to address issues or refusing to comply with accepted protocols. To understand types of behaviors that are truly intimidating goes beyond just the verbal abuse. The intimidating behavior is really what can upset individuals to the point that they are not able to do their job as they should, and it could potentially compromise patient care, quality, and patient safety.[2]

ESCALATION OF AN INCIDENT

If attempts to subdue the bully do not work, you may choose to escalate the situation, albeit carefully. You can raise your voice ever so slightly to convey your irritation to see how the bully will respond. If the bully then raises his voice, you can step closer. If the bully also steps closer, the bully is telling you, "This is not going to be easy. I am not going to back down from you in this environment." This is your signal to end the negotiation and leave.

Be aware of whether a person who has greater resources than you is a bully. Not all powerful people are bullies. If someone is just overly aggressive, you would treat that individual differently. You might even consider saying, "I'm perceiving your actions as being overly aggressive." The person says, "I'm sorry. That was not my intent" and changes his demeanor. A bully would say, "Yeah, so what?" That response lets you know you're dealing with a different type of person. Once you make that distinction from the behavior that you're sensing, and you confirm exactly what you're dealing with, you adjust your behavior.

Use this knowledge to your advantage when you are negotiating with a person or entity who is not a bully. If the individual is easy to deal with you can try to get concessions. Those concessions might not have been as feasible prior to you stating you are perceiving the other person as aggressive. See what the non-bully does with the concession you have asked for. The individual who is more easy-going may grant you the concession simply because he now wants to back up the words he just said ("That was not my intent"). He really means "My words are one thing, but let me show you by my actions that I mean what I say. I'll make that concession."

You may also decide to test the person who you know is a bully to see how aggressive he might become because you asked for him to make a concession.

"Why would I do that?" might be the bully's response.

You would respond, "Because it would be beneficial to our purpose in this negotiation."

Here's what you need to remember. The person who is asking the questions is the person in charge of the negotiation. If the bully then wants to know how that would be viewed as being positive, you need to shift the mindset of the bully. Take the question away from him and instead, pose a question to gain control of the negotiation. The exchange might look like this:

You: "Well don't you think so?"

The bully: "No, I don't."

You: "Why don't you think so?"

The bully: "Because it's rubbish."

You: "Why do you consider it to be rubbish?"

The bully: "Because it seems like it's more favorable to your position than mine."

You: "How is that?"

The bully: "Look at what you're proposing. . . ."

During the exchange you received more insight about the thoughts of the bully simply by asking questions. You had more control of the situation by doing so. That's a tactic that can be used in any negotiation with a bully. You can look at President Donald Trump and see how he attempts to bully everybody except Russian president Vladimir Putin. He will not do anything to go against Putin. Why? Because Putin has leverage. Anytime you can find the right leverage to use against a bully you will make him back down.

WATCHING FOR ESCALATION

Use clues to interpret the other negotiator's posture, the negotiating position, and his words to see if you can prevent an escalation of a negotiation during which there's no more discussion because there's no more communication. Observe his body language when he's making declarations. For example, if he's touching his chin with his forefinger and thumb, he's indicating he's in contemplative mode. If his fists are balled and his hands are down, he's displaying the degree of commitment to the discussion. If he's touching his heart, he's displaying sincerity. If he's rolling his eyes, it's skepticism. His mouth agape could be akin to surprise.

Use these signs to gain insight about his mindset. Watch his body language to see if you are in danger. If you see he has his fists balled and his hands are down, move away from him. Alternatively, you may want to show him that you're not fearful of backing down from him and then see what he does next. You can prevent aggressive action by the nature of your reaction. When you are watching his actions, you know what preventive measures to adopt.

The bully has his fists balled up; hypothetically, you could ball your fists up also. Both of you are now saying, "I'm going to become a little more aggressive and I'm ready." You can take charge of the situation if you think you are in a strong enough position to prevent him from escalating the negotiation. As you are balling your fists with your hands down by your side you can also take a step closer toward him. That would say, "I'm coming into your space. I'm not afraid of you at all."

If you saw him with balled fists, another preventive action could be to simply say, "I don't think this is the proper time for us to continue. Let's reconvene at another time." You will be preventing what could be an escalation to a point where you are trapped.

The body language gesture of his fists balled and hands down by his side is indicating he's losing the ability to be logical; emotion is taking control. His emotions may drive him to feel protective of his own interests, and they could be directing him to become more verbally or physically aggressive. In either case, that's not the mindset you want to negotiate with. Getting out of the environment protects your interests so that you don't make a hasty agreement or feel threatened.

Another way to change the environment is to start laughing if you think its appropriate for the situation. Laughter is contagious; he might start laughing too. You have changed the dynamics of the negotiation and prevented a possibly unpleasant situation from getting worse.

Listen for language that indicates the negotiation is escalating. The bully may say, "I don't think so," while snarling at you. Milder forms of this are, "This is not going to happen" and "This is my best offer." The bully may attempt to convince you he is more sincere than he is. But watch his actions and body language. Suppose he says, "This is my best offer" and then flashes a big smile at you when he says that. He's out of sync with his body language and words. Analyze what he says to see what his words mean to him. In certain environments it may be customary to speak very aggressively with someone just as a normal practice of the negotiation process.

Not only do you need to understand what is normal for him, but in so doing you know how to evaluate his mindset through his actions. You will have insight through the words he's using as to whether he's escalating or de-escalating the negotiation. Understand what word choices mean to him. If I say to you, "We have a deal," do I really mean that we have a deal or am I really saying we have a deal based on our most recent discussion but not the terms you discussed before that?

Ask probing questions to figure out the meaning of the agreement to a deal. Verify your understanding. "Can you tell me exactly what that means?" Let him give you his definition and then you have his perspective of what he's saying. You then also know the words that he uses mean "X" versus you constantly thinking those words mean "Y."

TARGETING THE VULNERABLE

The best time to negotiate with a bully is when he's the weakest and you're the strongest. Consider the situation of men in power who have forced girls, boys, women, or men to do things that they should not have been forced to do. As this book is being written there is a wave of women across the country who are coming forward to publicly call out powerful people for sexual harassment. The people speaking up are sometimes sharing their names. In other situations, they are anonymous. Some are discussing incidents that occurred years ago, while others are reporting recent events.

For example, at least six women alleged they were victims of sexual harassment by Florida-based Senator Jack Latvala, a Republican forced to stand down from until a Senate investigation is complete. "As long as Jack Latvala could be in control of a $83 billion budget, victims are going to be terrified to come forward," said Tiffany Cruz, the Tallahassee-based lawyer who filed a Senate complaint on behalf of a Senate staffer whose name remains anonymous.[2]

Cruz sent a letter to House Speaker Richard Corcoran accusing Latvala's son, Representative Chris Latvala, and his friend, Representative Kathleen Peters, of attempting to intimidate witnesses by being critical of the allegations on social media. She added:

Many women have chosen to remain anonymous due to legitimate fear for their safety and retaliation by the perpetrator. Rather than encouraging individuals who are victims of sexual harassment to come forward, anonymously or otherwise, they have taken to every avenue of social media to condemn the victims. Their actions are purely for intimidation, not for the public interest.[3]

Democrat Senator Lauren Book has a theory as to why no one in Tallahassee is willing to make their allegations public. "This is a male-dominated culture that has existed for a very long time with individuals who have been in power for a very long time. There are so many women who fear for their livelihood, fear for their reputation, in speaking out."[4]

The first report by a victim of bullying behavior may stimulate a wave of others to speak out, tipping the balance of power from the bully being powerful to the bully trying to hide from the spotlight. The victims' strength come from others who are supporting their effort, and conversely, the victim may continue to tolerate the bullying behavior because others around her say, "Don't speak up. You could lose your job." As Cruz explained, "There is zero political motivation behind why these women are making the accusations. Latvala is a man who collects a paycheck from the state of Florida. He is very wealthy. He has a lot of political power and the victims do not. The only people who are going to be crucified are the victims." Many in the Florida's capital say they believe there are others who have their own harassment tales about other current elected officials.[5]

Senator Latvala resigned in the face of a corruption investigation or possible expulsion.[6]

The stories of abuse hurled at the entertainment, political, tech, and other industries could represent a watershed moment to end tolerance of such behavior. The media has noticed that few women and men of color were involved in the dozens of complaints about rape or sexual harassment. Black, Asian-American, and immigrant women are often reticent to speak up about sexual harassment. Rutgers University historian

Deborah Gray White commented that in the days of slavery, black women's bodies were not their own and racist stereotypes were used to justify abuse. Black women have been perceived as promiscuous and available to all men. As a result, black women have had a harder time proving sexual exploitation. In response, many chose to be silent as a form of self-preservation.[7]

The Asian culture emphasizes not worrying parents and not sharing your family problems with others, says Anna Bang, education coordinator at KANB-WIN, a Chicago-based domestic violence and sexual assault services group. Women of Latin American descent are also stereotyped as being submissive and sexually available, according to Monica Russel y Rodriquez, a Northwestern University ethnographer. Undocumented women would be the least likely to report an assault for fear of unwanted attention.[8]

Young girls can also be targets of sexual assault. GOP candidate for the Senate Roy Moore of Alabama was accused of initiating sexual encounters with teenagers as young as 14 years old when he was a 32-year-old district attorney. Roy Moore denied the claims or said they were politically motivated.[9] He lost the election. As the victims watch and wait for the proper time to come forward, they need to consider when they are the strongest and the bully is the weakest. They can gather additional information if they want to launch a misdirection campaign.

TIMING

The timing of a negotiation is extremely important. I'll use the situation that I experienced several times throughout my life when purchasing an automobile. First, I gathered all the background information about the manufacturer's cost and the types of deals the car dealership would offer on automobiles. I would find out when they would offer sales and how much they were willing to concede on price and then all a sudden turn around and try to upsell you on something else that had a higher margin for them.

I did all of that and then waited until they were at their weakest or most vulnerable: the end of the month when quotas had to be made. By using the timing of waiting until the end of the month, I was positioning myself as somewhat of a savior to them. "I'll throw you a lifeline, but you have to offer me the type of deal I need for me to purchase the vehicle."

Timing plays a key role because it can also sway an individual based on the amount of power he perceives he has in a situation. Suppose a negotiator knows he must have a deal concluded or else he's going to lose his job or is at risk for losing a big customer. Time is getting ready to run out on closing the deal. He is willing to make a deal to save his job.

We always need to be mindful of the timing of any negotiation because the timing will also dictate to what degree someone is weaker or stronger based on when the negotiation is taking place.

VISUAL CUES

Visual cues convey information about the perceived strength of the negotiator.

For example, a woman's husband was entitled to have a company car and had some leeway regarding the choice of the car. She wanted to sit in a similar car in a local dealership before he made his final decision. She had a young baby at the time. She walked in holding her son after getting dressed in a hurry. She had pulled on a pair of pants inside out, which she did not realize until it was too late. The car salesman dismissed her when she walked into the building looking a little disheveled and holding her infant. Finally, he realized she wasn't going to leave and he wandered over. She said, "I am here to pick out the model of the company car that my husband wants to order from your dealership." He had a whole different demeanor at that point.

I've used a ploy of walking into a Mercedes dealership in dressed-down clothes. I did not want to convey the fact that I had a lot of money because I didn't want the car salesman with whom I was negotiating to think, "I'll charge him an extra $10,000 and see if I can get away with it."

You must always know what you're dealing with before you attempt to deal with it.

Knowing Your Negotiation Objective

I remember getting a call once from someone who was looking for an individual to come in and do a presentation on negotiation tactics, strategies, and how to read body language. When I inquired as to what it was that they wanted, the dialogue went like this:

Caller: "I don't know. I'm just trying to get how much it would cost."
Me: "It's not a cost, it's an investment."
Caller: "I was told just to get the cost."
Me: "How long would you like someone to speak?"
Caller: "I don't know. I was just told to get the cost."
Me: "How many people will actually be there?"
Caller: "I'm not exactly sure. I was just told. . . ."

The point I'm making is that person was negotiating on behalf of someone in the organization. The person who made the assignment directed the helper to find out the cost, as if that was the only factor the individual had to evaluate. In that case they were losing out on what a good speaker is versus a so-so speaker, a content speaker versus a generalist; and that's the point when you're also talking about negotiations. You must understand who will be representing you in a negotiation. You may be overlooking factors that will aid in the negotiation with a bully.

Strength of the Negotiators

Suppose you need to decide which of your team members will be up against a bully. You know in advance that the other negotiator is going to perform bullying tactics against your team. Consider sending out either a weaker or stronger negotiator in what you can call Phase 1. You get an idea of how the bully is going to interact with your team player if the bully was negotiating against a weaker person or a stronger person. This trial run gives you the insight to modify your negotiation position ever so slightly.

You must always be mindful of with whom you are negotiating and that person's mindset, and that you must possess the right mindset. Defining the right mindset for the environment is important because not only are you always negotiating, but you're also influencing what is going to occur after that phase of the interaction.

I know there are days that you wake up and you feel more vulnerable and fragile than usual. Other days you wake up and feel powerful and energized. Your mindset affects your negotiations when you are anticipating that person is going to be more powerful. If you wake up thinking the other person is more powerful that becomes your reality. Your perspective is, "I'm less powerful in this situation," and that will manifest itself in your negotiation. Yes, you may be less powerful in an encounter with a bully. Knowing that gives you the opportunity to buttress the lack of power by finding resources you can use to strengthen yourself before you enter the negotiation. Strike a power pose to get yourself pumped up. In addition, when you think you are in a less-than-powerful position, you need to examine why you have such feelings.

The mindset you have before and during a negotiation will determine the way the negotiation plays out. It affects the strategies you use, the concessions you make, and the way you allow yourself to be pushed around. The way to offset all of that is to anticipate what might occur in the negotiation and to what degree you might be bulled. You can then address or prevent all those bullying tactics by making sure you have resources at the ready that you can utilize to communicate that you are not as powerless as you may appear to be.

The persona you project is also important. If you have the attitude of "I'm great" even if it's not true, that will become your reality. Show that through your body language gestures like standing with your hands on your hips. This conveys your defiance about pursuing a course of action the bully demands. Your body language says, "I'm going to dig my heels in. I'm not going to be as mobile as you would want me to be. Now bring it on."

The attitude that you *display* reveals the attitude you *possess*. The bully will see the signals and will likely push you around if you don't convey strength.

President Trump does not push President Putin, but he does push other foreign leaders because he has this attitude that he's great, he's wonderful, and he's here to "Make America Great Again," yet he still won't push back on Putin. Listen to his words, but watch his actions even more because those actions will tell you the mindset of the person with whom you're negotiating.

Pay attention to your language when you are conveying your strength: "I won't" as opposed to "Maybe I will." Or "This is not going to occur" versus "This might have a chance."

Mind the intonation and the inflection in your voice when you pronounce your words. "This is *not* going to happen" communicates more conviction than "Well maybe this can happen."

BODY LANGUAGE

If someone says, "Maybe we can do this" while rubbing her thigh, take note of that. Not only is she not overly sure of what she's saying but she's trying to comfort herself, which lends more credibility to the fact that she's not sure. That also means if you were bullying her in that instance, you can push her even harder than you have been. Listen for the words that are being used and how they are being used: "Maybe we might be able to" versus a definitive "No, this is not going to happen." Watch out for the body language gestures of comforting oneself when one is speaking these words.

Listen to the bully's tone and consistency of his words with his body language. For example, suppose he says, "I'm going to beat the snot out of you in this negotiation" as he's stepping back from you. He's saying, "I'm not going to beat the snot out of you or at least if I choose to do so there's going to be some distance between the two of us." That means there may be a delay before his aggression escalates.

These nonverbal clues are insights into his real thought process; watch his body language. If he aggressively snarls at you while he's leaning in and says, "You take this damn deal or else I'm walking," watch his hands. He may have his forefinger and thumb pressed together on his left hand while he was saying that. That gesture is a sign of preciseness.

Observing body language signals the opposing negotiator makes during such a declaration gives you the insight to his degree of conviction about what he is saying.

Let's talk about other comfort gestures. He says to you in a slightly different tone, "You better take this deal or else I'm going to leave." Instead of that gesture of the forefinger and a thumb being placed together, he's rubbing his hands. He's saying through that gesture, "I think you're really going to take this deal because you perceive me as being serious" and rubbing his hands in anticipation.

Let's look at a different position. He says the same thing but instead of rubbing his hands he's wringing his hands. Now through wringing his hands he's saying, "You know I may be really bluffing you at this time to see exactly what you're going to do. If you get up and start to walk away I may have to do something to pull you back to the negotiation table."

Consider how the bully has used the same word with different tones and body language gestures. The gestures associated with those same words had a different meaning. If you are an astute negotiator, you have much greater insight into the degree and emphasis the words have and what action that negotiator may be ready to engage in next.

Note the bully's gestures and actions. Is he a softcore bully in waiting (meaning he's just trying to feel his way through)? Is he a real bully who is aggressive because he really doesn't want to negotiate with you to the degree that you're not willing to make concessions? If the latter is the case and he displays body language gestures I've already described, you will have insight as to why he may not want to negotiate with you.

When you are face to face, observe whether his feet are pointed directly to yours. This says, "I'm still engaged" versus one foot turned in one direction, which says, "I'm going to exit the conversation, I'm going to exit the negotiation, and I'm going to move away." If he is trying to bully you and he has one foot pointed away from you, he is displaying through that gesture that he's not as intent about bullying you as he is saying.

Body language is an integral part of the words being exchanged simply because they will communicate additional meaning. In Chapter 3, I covered micro-expressions, those fleeting indicators of attitude, mood, and thoughts. If you can spot the bully's micro-expressions during a negotiation, you see the snapshot of what's occurring in the bully's mind. If the bully says, "Take it or leave it" and smiles at you, that's a mixed message versus the bully's face showing contempt.

Contempt is displayed by one corner of the lip being turned up versus the person saying, "You can take it or leave it" while grimacing to show, "I don't like you. Take it or leave it. I want to be done with this negotiation. I've had enough of you. You are trying my patience and I want to get my way." Your response is to get up to walk away from the table while saying, "I guess I'll leave it." Suddenly, the bully's mouth drops open for a moment in surprise. That will give you insight that this person is shocked. He does not want you to walk away.

The bully says, "I'm going to beat your butt" and you step closer to the bully. Watch the bully's eyes. When the bully widens his eyes, that gesture is telling you the bully was somewhat surprised that you displayed the nerve to walk toward the bully. The bully could display fear by starting to back away from you. That means the bully was posturing to get you to back down and thinks he is stronger than he is to see exactly how you would respond to his gesture.

If you're able to pick all of that up in the negotiation, it gives you a much stronger sense from which to negotiate. You also get insight into how well the strategy you have crafted for the negotiation is working in real time. You have done something to respond, which was part of your plan for the negotiation. Now you have direct feedback and validity as to what it is just by glimpsing the micro-expression occurring in the negotiation.

PSYCHOLOGICAL PLOYS

We sometimes use ploys in a reflexive way, without even being aware of what we are doing. For example, you may feign weakness or strength depending upon what the situation calls for.

Carter Page, an advisor to President Trump, was questioned in the investigation into Russia tampering with the U.S. elections. The administration wanted to distance itself from him and make him appear less important.

One of the strategies Carter adopted was to be careful in answering questions. He was evasive and difficult to follow in his testimony.

He responded to questions by saying things like, "I really can't give an honest answer to that because if by chance I have forgotten something, and it's discovered later you will say that I'm lying."[10] Now is he sly or smart? One would have to consider that when negotiating with him, but he also has the demeanor of being docile, someone you would never think would have the level of importance that he had with the administration. As of this writing he has not been indicted.

You can feign not only weakness or strength, but you can appear to be disheveled, and all those personas will give you some form of leverage when dealing with the opposing negotiator from a psychological perspective.

One time around Christmas I stopped my car at the light and there was a big bus that was making a turn. Apparently, the bus driver did see me, but at the same time he was trying to make me back up, pull to the side, or do something to give him more room. He came extremely close to my car. I lowered my window. I was getting ready to express my exasperation when he rolled down his window and said "Merry Christmas!" with a big smile on his face. That changed my whole demeanor. It took the wind out of my sails.

Those are the types of psychological ploys you can employ when dealing with a bully or anyone. When you're doing so with a bully you have to be somewhat mindful of how he will take it. If he feels as though you are humiliating him in front of others, that may cause him to escalate the situation with statements such as, "You think that was funny? Let me show you what funny is in a negotiation." Or "So, you think you got the better of me in the last segment of our negotiation? Let me show you what will happen this time around."

Be mindful of the acts you engage in and the type of responses from the bully they'll likely provoke. Psychological ploys are advantageous tools. You should always plan how you're going to use them in a negotiation.

STOPPING THE CYCLE

Victims will remain targets until the cycle of bullying stops. The most clear-cut example of this is the cycle that occurs in domestic violence. As an example, a man who drank too much becomes aggressive and hits his partner. He feels remorse and promises her it will never happen again. Then the tension builds, he drinks, he hits her, and the cycle repeats. The cycle stops when the woman can get far away from the bully.

The college fraternity culture endorses bullying in the form of hazing. Several deaths of young men have drawn attention to the need to change the environment in which dangerous behavior occurs. The deaths have typically been due to elevated blood alcohol levels. But other bullying behavior occurs, including racist hazing of sorority women, anti-Semitic jokes, and continually taunting of freshmen by upper classmen. Schools have responded to the deaths by suspending or terminating the chapters' charters. But lasting change must occur from within by changing the perception of the behavior to one that is unacceptable.

Elizabeth Allen, a professor at University of Maine, says, "Creating and enforcing policy only goes so far in changing the culture. . . . Visible leadership from administrators, student organizations, and anyone who has the courage to stand up and step up, makes a huge difference."[11]

Women who feel they are victims of sexual harassment may file a claim with the U.S. Equal Employment Opportunity Commission. The director of the EEOC Tampa Florida field office gave an example of a scenario that involved warehouse workers who hung posters of scantily clad women along the walls. This offended some coworkers and can be construed as sexual harassment. The EEOC website allows victims to file complaints online. The EEOC looks for evidence that proves repeated, unwanted advances and requests for sexual favors that cause discomfort in the work environment. Employers cannot sit back and wait for complaints. They need to be proactive and take preventative measures against sexual harassment. They should know what to do if an employee crosses the line. Speaking up and reporting these incidents is the only way to change the workplace culture.[12]

Zero tolerance of this activity sends a message to others thinking of carrying out similar behavior. Dr. Alan Rosenstein works with healthcare organizations to correct bullying behavior. He outlines what stops the behavior: The organization itself, the culture, the leadership, middle management, front line management, and staff all must recognize how important this really is and to be committed to doing something about it. That's crucial.[13]

You need to have the leadership, provide programs, endorse the programs, support the people who are doing the right things, and not tolerate the individuals who are doing the wrong things. As part of the organizational commitment through the culture and the leadership, the second thing is to raise the business case of why this is so important. To give you stereotypical bully physicians' reaction, they know they are yelling at somebody. It's the way they have always done business. They will forget it as soon as it is over, and they can get on and do what they do. If necessary, they will say they are sorry. They just don't see that when you have done it forty times, nobody is going to want to work with you.

In fact, it can result in other staff being so antagonized that they won't correct the physician bully if they see the physician doing something wrong or call the physician for a clarification of an order or a need because the patient needs attention.

The first adjustment is a cultural commitment; the second intervention is to raise the levels of awareness of why this is such a significant issue, particularly on staff communication and patient outcomes of care. Everybody is in the business of having a successful patient outcome.

They just do not see the downstream effect.

The third piece is to provide education. Some of it is generic education on patient safety and adverse events, and a lot of it has to do with diversity training, sensitivity training, conflict management, assertiveness training, team collaboration, and communication tools. The result is improving patient outcomes of care. So rather than taking the confrontational approach ("You jerk! You should never do this. Why did you do this? Don't ever do it again or else!") the healthcare team must look at ways to prevent these types of things from happening.[14]

You need to have the right frame of mind when negotiating with anyone, including with a bully. The right perspective puts you on the right track from which to engage with the bully. The bully will take advantage of you if your mindset is not attuned to the dynamics of the negotiation.

The right mindset is appropriate for the situation and so you must plan for what type of persona you're going to project. If the bully despises weakness, you do not want to reveal a demeanor that portrays you are weak. If the bully happens to be someone who will be more easy-going or will acquiesce to someone who is more powerful, you want to position yourself in the best possible light so that he views you as a worthy opponent.

Bullies don't go up against those who are stronger than themselves because the bully does not want to be belittled in front of others. Also take into consideration how you might solicit the support of others. The Code Pink maneuver can also form a more robust opponent for the bully to confront. In doing so you will have deterred the bully from engaging in acts of aggression.

IN CONCLUSION

Differentiate between a bully who may be controlling versus bullying. Some people don't see themselves as bullies. They may be the type who likes to be in control of situations and displays overly aggressive means to maintain that control. The two perspectives possess different mindsets.

Identify the personality type of the bully you're negotiating with. Thus, even in your first encounter with a person (and after that time), you should assess that person's traits, demeanor, and characteristics. Doing so will give you the insight needed to formulate a negotiation strategy.

Determine the best environment to negotiate with a bully. He may be stronger in one environment as the result of resources surrounding him or those he must save face for; this may also tend to make him cockier than he'd normally be. If that's the case, get him out of his environment; this should be done physically or psychologically. In doing so you'll dilute his psychological powers and weaken him mentally in the process (that is, power is perceptional).

If addressing a bully on a one-on-one basis doesn't achieve your objectives, marshal forces to use as leverage against him. Depending on the situation, let those who he has more respect for take the lead on your behalf. Never let a bully know how strong your forces are.

You must be prepared to send in a second, third, and fourth wave who are stronger than those who precede them. For maximum effect, the timing of your next foray should occur just when the bully thinks he's squashed your best efforts. In normal situations, over time you'll wear the bully down and he'll acquiesce to your wishes. Be mindful of the bully who won't acquiesce over a period of exhaustive negotiations when forces have been marshaled against him. You might be dealing with a bully who's willing to destroy himself for the sake of denying you any kind of victory.

To prevent yourself from making too many concessions, establish exit points that indicate when you should depart the negotiation. Always be mindful that the longer you stay engaged in a negotiation, the likelier you are to make concessions to your disadvantage. This is due to the psychological need to see the negotiation to its end. This could be to your severe detriment.

Once you've achieved your objectives, over time re-engage the bully from a polite perspective and observe how he interacts with you. To the degree the relationship is important to you, be prepared to let him win an encounter, but never let him bully you again. Your prior actions should be engrained in his mind to the point that he'd not want to re-experience the same type of negotiation.

As further insight into the effects your engagement has had with a bully, note how those closest to the bully engage with you after an encounter. Their actions will allow you to assess the degree of sting that still resides in the bully.

Bullies only pick on those that they perceive to be weaker than themselves. Don't let a bully perceive weakness in you and he'll have no target to attack—and everything will be right with the world.

HOMEWORK

Go back and look at the homework assignments from each chapter. Over the next seven weeks, choose one assignment to pay special attention to. If you don't reach a point of comfort with any topic, address it again.

As you go through this exercise, you'll increase your ability to negotiate better, and to identify the types and styles of bullies. In the process, you will have gained knowledge and insight that will propel you to greater heights in life.

Notes

CHAPTER 1

1. Jouet, M. Trump Didn't Invent "Make America Great Again," How conservatives hijacked the idea of American exceptionalism. *Mother Jones*, January/February 2017.

2. Melton, Marissa, Is "Make America Great Again" Racist? VOA, August 31, 2017

3. *www.aljazeera.com/news/2017/08/unite-white-supremacists-rally-virginia-170812142356688.html*

4. *www.cnn.com/2017/08/31/us/georgia-cobb-county-officer-racial-comment-trnd/index.html*

5. *www.merriam-webster.com/dictionary/bully*

6. Dr. Kristin Williams-Washington, personal communication, December 29, 2017.

7. Ibid.

8. *www.wikihow.com/Spot-a-Sociopath.*

9. *https://en.wikipedia.org/wiki/Sexual_predator*

10. *TIME Magazine*, 190 no. 16–17 (2017): 28–31.

11. "The Harvey Weinstein Scandal: Taking down a predator," *People Magazine*, October 30, 2017, 49.

12. Ibid.

13. *www.miamiherald.com/news/politics-government/state-politics/article190803584.html*

14. *https://en.wikipedia.org/wiki/Napoleon_complex.*

15. Dr. Kristin Williams-Washington, personal communication, December 29, 2017.

14. Ibid.

Chapter 2

1. *http://hnmcp.law.harvard.edu/hnmcp/blog/trumps-losing-negotiation-strategy/*

2. *www.usatoday.com/story/news/politics/2017/09/19/trump-we-have-no-choice-but-totally-destroy-north-korea-if-continues-nuclear-path/680329001/*

3. *http://www.colorado.edu/conflict/peace/treatment/prui7539.htm*

4. *Wintour, A. Leading the Way, Vogue, March 2018, p. 164.*

5. *www.cnn.com/2017/10/24/us/carlos-bell-maryland-hiv-coach/index.html*

6. *www.cnn.com/2017/12/07/us/larry-nassar-usa-gymnastics-sentence/index.html; www.usatoday.com/story/sports/olympics/2017/10/18/olympic-gold-medalist-mckayla-maroney-says-she-victim-sexual-abuse/774970001/*

7. *www.latimes.com/politics/washington/la-na-essential-washington-updates-trump-says-comey-better-hope-there-are-1494595058-htmlstory.html.*

8. *http://thehill.com/homenews/administration/336925-comey-lordy-i-hope-there-are-tape*

CHAPTER 3

1. *www.youtube.com/watch?v=1DwijJfVbBg*
2. *https://history.state.gov/milestones/1961-1968/cuban-missile-crisis*
3. *www.history.com/news/mussolinis-final-hours-70-years-ago*

CHAPTER 4

1. *www.aeaweb.org/conference/2018/preliminary/paper/A2EQbrKe*
2. *www.governing.com/gov-data/safety-justice/police-department-officer-demographics-minority-representation.htm*
3. *https://en.wikipedia.org/wiki/William_Shockley*
4. *www.theatlantic.com/business/archive/2015/05/the-financial-perks-of-being-tall/393518/*
5. *www.pitt.edu/~dash/type1620.html#andersen*
6. *www.justice.gov/usam/criminal-resource-manual-932-provisions-handling-qui-tam-suits-filed-under-false-claims-act*
7. *www.aclu.org/blog/free-speech/employee-speech-and-whistleblowers/never-run-when-youre-right-real-story-nypd*
8. *https://courses2.cit.cornell.edu/sociallaw/student_projects/DrivingWhileBlack.htm.*
9. *https://oureverydaylife.com/characteristics-female-bully-8466459.html*

CHAPTER 5

1. "I was sexually harassed by my professor," People, August 7, 2017, page 78-80.
2. Griffin M. Teaching cognitive rehearsal as a shield for lateral violence: an intervention for newly licensed nurses. *J Contin Educ Nurs.* 2004; 35 (6): 257-263.

3. www.jointcommission.org/sentinel_event_alert_issue_40_behaviors_that_undermine_a_culture_of_safety/

4. Dr. Alan Rosenstein, Bullying, Avoid Medical Errors, 2011.

5. www.cnn.com/2017/11/01/health/utah-nurse-officer-arrest-settlement-trnd/index.html

6. Dr. Alan Rosenstein, Bullying, Avoid Medical Errors, 2011.

7. https://oureverydaylife.com/characteristics-female-bully-8466459.html

8. YouTube's Style Queen, People, July 10, 2017, page 79.

9. Sarah Hyland fighting body bullies, People August 7, 2017 page 30.

10. www.washingtonexaminer.com/bill-oreilly-paid-32-million-for-sexual-harassment-settlement-in-january-one-month-before-he-resigned/article/2638263

CHAPTER 6

1. Graydon Carter, "The good, the bad and the truly, meaningfully dangerous," Vanity Fair, December 2017, 40-41.

2. Mary Ellen Klas, Sexual harassment claims against Sen. Latvala are still anonymous, Bradenton Herald, November 17, 2017, 5A.

3. Ibid.

4. Ibid.

5. www.miamiherald.com/news/politics-government/state-politics/article190803584.html

6. Ibid.

7. Few women of color in wave of accusers, Associated Press, Tampa Bay Times, November 19, 2017, 2A

8. Ibid.

9. http://time.com/5029172/roy-moore-accusers/

10. *www.vox.com/policy-and-politics/2017/11/7/16616912/cart-er-page-testimony-trump-russia* *https://www.washingtonpost.com/blogs/compost/wp/2017/11/07/the-paranoid-carter-page-transcript-what-in-gods-name-did-i-just-read/?utm_term=.ce236d39c454*

11. Alex Harris, After pledges' deaths and bad behavior, fraternity system is 'hanging by a thread', Bradenton Herald, November 17, 2017, 7A.

12. Ryan Callihan, Experts outline steps to combat sexual harassment at work, Bradenton Herald, November 17, 2017, p1A.

13. Dr. Alan Rosenstein, Bullying, Avoid Medical Errors, 2011.

14. Ibid.

Index